THE SOULS
OF
POOR FOLK

Alexander Irvine

THE SOULS
OF
POOR FOLK

APPLETREE PRESS
BELFAST

First published in 1921 by W. Collins, Sons & Co Ltd

This edition published in 1981 by
The Appletree Press Ltd
7 James Street South
Belfast BT2 8DL

ISBN 0 90465186 X

British Library Cataloguing in Publication Data
Irvine Alexander
The souls of poor folk
1. Antrim (Northern Ireland) — Social Life and customs — 19th century
I. Title
941.6'12081   DA 995.A/

ISBN 0-904651-86-X

Printed in Northern Ireland by
The Appletree Press Ltd

To Dorothy

In grateful remembrance of
other nights in other
chimney corners

Contents

Introduction

Among Ireland's most famous women was one who, amid the straitened circumstances of Ulster's mid-Victorian poor folk, desperately battled to keep alive the bodies and souls of those she loved. Anna Irvine spent her life 'at the bottom of the world' finely transmuting closed minds and shut hearts. In this sequel to her son's famous and well-loved tributary book, Dr Alexander Irvine returns his readers to 'that poor little chimney corner where My Lady— skilled in the anatomy of misfortune—sent forth light and healing to those in need.'

'The Souls of Poor Folk' was written during a trans-Atlantic voyage in the summer of 1920, a few weeks after Dr Irvine had paid what he believed would be his final visit to his Irish homeland. Fifty years after he had run shoeless, hatless and in rags through the streets of Antrim, his hometown, he observed, was changing—almost as utterly as it has changed in the half century since. With good humour, though not withholding any blemishes in those whom he loved. Irvine spent that voyage dreaming fondly and writing warmly about the poor folk he had known and loved best:

A new spirit, the spirit of the times, is making itself felt, and great changes are imminent. It is largely because of that, that I am going back to the period I know best to make a few more footnotes to the history of my people.

As a boy, when he scratched in the dunghills and gutters for scraps of meat, vegetables and refuse, he had had some misgivings about the distribution of the good things in life. Now, with the grown wisdom of the adult, his heart, mind and soul raged against the bludgeoning of the subservient poor which leads to an effacement of their spirit. All his life, Alexander Irvine fought and suffered for the well-being of the poorest of the poor upon whose back are always borne the world's heaviest burdens.

Tragically, the wisdom that imbued this mother's simple non-aligned religion appears as unpalatable in much of Ulster today as it was in the Irvines' Antrim of the 1870s:

Catholics and Protestants had no dealings with each other. They were further apart than the Jews and Samaritans were . . . We hated each other's religion and became irritated at every public expression of it . . . We were blind to our own shortcomings.

Even the cynical Willie Withero observed: 'Hate is surely ov the divil, and is the curse ov Ireland. They haavn't th' common sinse ov a banty hen who cyant see it.'

However, one should not give the impression that this is, primarily, a grave or serious book. Irvine had what Yeats called the power of very delicate spiritual writing. Here we have a rich complex of stories, full of fun and good humour, and a superb evocation of childhood:

10

Between my seventh and fourteenth birthdays was the magic period of my youth in Antrim. I used to think of those years as wasted time . . . I think differently now. I was idly dreaming, getting acquainted with life: the life of birds and beasts, of men and women, of trees and flowers.

The opening chapters colourfully recall the routine of daily life for the young Alexander—driving rooks from crops, swimming in the mill race, peddling newspapers—and the folk who made up his little world—the baker, grocer, blacksmith—all graphically captured in a memorable series of pen portraits. Here, for example, we meet old Antrim's Process Server, 'with his beaver slightly tilted to one side and his wellingtons (which) got in each other's way'. In moving the soul of the old drunken stonemason, John McConkey, Alexander reveals the first stirring within him of that inclination to serve his fellow men which, for him, was the highest conception of service to God.

The Bog-Queen's Flittin' is one of his Celtic mother's spell-binding chimney corner folktales. The magic charm of the seanachie (story-teller) before the glow of the peat fire of a long winter's night is vividly recreated. Full of local colour, it deftly blends fantasy and reality which, it not a panacea for destitution, diverted attention from it for a spell. 'To doubt the reality of the world of fancy through which she led us,' mused Irvine, 'would have been to doubt our own existence.'

While fact and fancy may share the same validity in the imagination, they can prove a troublesome mix in the real world. *A Corner in Larks* and, more profoundly, *The Miracle* record lessons learned

11

during the complicated days of adolescence. In the latter, under the guiding hand of his New Testament mother, Alexander, shouldering a sackful of stolen potatoes, attains a spiritual milestone when he draws an inescapable parallel with Christian labouring under his sackful of sins.

As they grew to manhood, one by one Anna's sons—William, James, Dan and Alexander—went 'over the hills and far away'. The story of her first prodigal, however, for whom she placed a *Candle in the Window*—a potent symbol—demonstrates the heavy penalties exacted when pride leads one to violate the Fifth Commandment.

Anna used *The Coming of the Lamp* to melt away her husband's obstinacy and pride. The lion, Jamie, sees his home—once again!—'bathed in glory' by the lamb.

The penultimate chapter treats the reader to the conviviality of a homely debate on 'the oddities of quare people' which is conducted by an assembly of local Solomons gathered in the Irvine's chimney corner community centre. Anna observes their minds working, when they work at all. With subtle doses of mental medicine, she points a moral and finds God in the souls of the poor folk.

The book closes quietly with a study of 'himself', that illiterate Protestant shoemender whom Anna chose as her soul's companion. Jamie Irvine had his faults, chiefly those of truculence and pride, but at heart he was a good man, devoted to his wife and sharing her religious grasp of the principal human need for love in both family and public life. When Jamie had Anna, she had him and both of them had God. Inevitably there came a time when the light went out of his life: Anna died of tuberculosis and a desolate loneliness permeated the old home. Finally, Jamie followed. The love they shared remained true through life to death. By their example, Alexander began to see:

> If we love for what we can get out of the loved one, if our affection has an ulterior motive, we become the architects of our own destruction. The love that lasts—the only love with any chance of permanency—is love that is based on friendship. The surface of the sea of love is strewn with derelicts. They were beautiful ships when they left the harbour but they were not built for the storm.

Dr Irvine's stories continue to live in readers' affections not for their anecdotal elements but because of the characters that inhabit them, the authentic sense of atmosphere and the insights they offer into our human conditions.

Anna, Jamie, Alexander and all the poor folk of this little volume have long since departed. Pogue's Entry survives, a salutary reminder of our need to accommodate that kind of love which once shone from its poverty corner:

> 'Ah, friends beloved,' said Anna, 'we all know . . . the world is hard up for maany things jist now, but it's harder up for love and kindness than for anything else. For folks in the flesh around here let us pray for a large distribution of the Father's love and dear knows even poor craithers away in the mind could tell ye that—LOVE IS ENOUGH.'

Alastair Smyth
Antrim

Chapter 1

OVER THE HILLS AND FAR AWAY

But I, being poor have only my dreams,
I spread my dreams under your feet;
Tread softly because you tread on my dreams.

W. B. Yeats

I

Nobody but an Ulsterman can understand the Ulster mind, and an Ulsterman is never more than half convinced that he knows himself. The farther away we get, the closer the view and the more accurate the judgement. When I returned to Antrim after an absence of a generation, I felt as if I were entering an unknown town in an unknown land.

In the old days, when information was less accessible than today, 'over the hills and far away' was the expression that answered a multitude of questions about the outside world. Our hopes and aspirations were all to be realised, 'over the hills and far away'. That was where great things happened. That was where everybody had work and enough to eat.

'What will ye do whin yer a maan, dear?' my mother asked me when I was five, and I answered, 'Oh, I'm goin' over the hills an' far away.'

Then there came a time, long years afterwards, when Antrim itself, with all its tender and sacred associations, became to me, 'over the hills and far away!'

On my return I found changes at the top and changes at the bottom of social life. My old town still lingers in the rear of the march of progress, but it has changed. Even the poorest of the poor have enough to eat. That may seem commonplace to some. To me it was vital.

A political meeting had been held. That was an innovation. It was the only one I ever heard of being held there. It was an indication of a change of mind. I was sceptical that I would live to see that day. As a result of that meeting a Labour candidate was returned at the head of the polls for a local office. That was a revolution. In the days of my youth capacity or desire for either political analysis or social criticism was unthinkable.

Loyalty to the *status quo* used to be a fetish with us, submission to authority was our eleventh commandment and discontent was treason or worse. A new spirit, the spirit of the times, is making itself felt, and great changes are imminent. It is largely because of that, that I am going back to the period I know best to make a few more footnotes to the history of my people.

Poor as we were in those mid-Victorian days, we considered ourselves amongst the elect. Yet I well remember how nimbly and instinctively I hopped out of a policeman's line of vision as a sparrow hops out of the way of a motor-car in the crowded city streets.

Policemen, gamekeepers, and watchmen were our natural enemies. We had a right on public highways, but were only half convinced of that. The moment we stepped off the street or the highway we were trespassers.

In my childish heart there grew a hatred— an implacable hatred against the high stone walls that hid from our view the lake and the woods. I saw it a few weeks ago, and I hated it with a fiercer hatred than I did when a boy. I am told it was built during the great famine in order to provide work. Better a thousand times that a thousand men should die of starvation than that their children and children's children should be starved of that view which belongs to them!

A wise man once described poverty as 'the sepulchre of brave designs'. But we had no designs. We did have occasional longings for something larger and better but they flickered out before they got any hold upon us. We had subservient minds and gave without grudge whatever respect was demanded of us. 'Our betters' was no mere empty phrase. It had the sanction of religion, and was to us a religious duty. It never occurred to us that respect might have a reciprocal relation. We expected nothing, and getting it, were not disappointed.

The great institutions of our town were, the church, the pub, the court-house, and the pawnshop. With the pub and the court-house I had no personal experience, but the church and the pawnshop I knew well. The art of the town was centred in the church, and apart from the church services, the church itself had a refining influence. Of course, there were crowds of us who never entered it after Baptism, but to those of us who did, it was a power in the creation of ideals and the formation of character.

My mind being a little ahead of my social status, I pushed myself into situations from which I was forced to retire. Even when I acquired boots and a paper collar I was too conspicuous by the scantiness of my outfit to get the full benefit.

Illiteracy was a further handicap. Added to that I

17

was an inveterate asker of questions. I helped old John McConkey to organise a temperance society. I had done all the work; John, himself, was my first convert. When we gathered around a table to elect officers John informed me that I couldn't be elected to any of the 'main offices'.

'Why?' I asked, with a guilty feeling, as if I had been caught red-handed drinking whisky. John looked at me. He had only one eye but it was full of tender solicitude and pity for me.

'Bekase,' said he, 'yer too d——d ignorant, m' bhoy!'

I acknowledged the truth of the charge and nominated John for president.

Catholics and Protestants had no dealings with each other. They were farther apart than the Jews and Samaritans were. I cannot remember a single instance in which the people of Antrim met as citizens or townspeople. We hated each other's religion and became irritated at every public expression of it. There was no neutral ground upon which the majority and the minority could meet.

Only in retrospect and from a distance does one discover that the scheme of things left much to be desired. In it and of it there is nothing unusual. We were blind to our own shortcomings.

And yet my dearest chum was a Roman Catholic. We never discussed politics or religion—each was sure in his own mind that the other would be ultimately damned. We had an occasional good-natured cross-fire of banter and humorous ridicule, but never a serious discussion.

'Where wuz yer religion before oul Henry th' Eighth?' he would say, and having no strong defence for 'Oul Henry', I would reply: 'Where wuz yer face before it wuz washed?'

The percentage of those who were chronically hungry in our community was small. My people were of that percentage, and yet we never whined over our lot. We did not view the world through stained-glass windows, neither did we see it, as my mother would say, 'through dirty specs'.

We were happy-go-lucky folks, taking the smiles of good fortune or the bludgeonings of chance just as they came, without undue elation or depression.

II

'Sir,' said Dr Johnson, in answering Hume, who believed that those who were happy were equally happy, 'that those who are happy are equally happy is not true. A peasant and a philosopher may be equally satisfied, but not equally happy. Happiness consists in the multiplicity of agreeable conscious-ness. A peasant has not a capacity for equal happiness with a philosopher.'

When Johnson talked about peasants he was guessing. He knew little about them and that little was of a second-hand variety. A philosopher may have a super-normal capacity for happiness and be as miserable as the devil. Outsiders imagine 'the man below' has a good time, generally, in Ireland, but we always looked upon him as the most miserable of beings.

It isn't what we possess that counts; it's the use we make of our possessions, and a big use of a few capacities is better than a small use of a great number.

Sir Walter Scott tells a story of an Eastern Caliph who was advised by his physician to find a happy man and wear his shirt as a cure for ennui.

Depairing of finding such a man in his own unhappy land, he made a tour of Europe. Italy, France, and Spain were covered without results. In England he found John Bull quarrelling and grousing over the high cost of living. In Scotland they were having a shindy over theology, so he crossed to Ireland. The fed-up monarch was convinced at once that the Irish were the happiest people in the world. One day he heard a man singing in the fields as he worked. The psychological moment had arrived. 'Seize him! seize him!' said the excited man. His retainers at once seized Pat and stripped him, but alas! the happy man was without a shirt!

If Dr Johnson's 'multiplicity of agreeable consciousness' be rated at one hundred, by what percentage would that maximum be reduced—in his own case—by lack of a shirt? Probably fifty per cent. In the case of an Irish peasant the reduction would be about five per cent. In my own case it would have been about two and a half.

Are there any scales by which can be weighed and the difference determined, between the joy, pleasure, or happiness experienced by W. G. Grace in a cricket match and that experienced by a ragged peasant boy who plays with pot-sticks for wickets and a fence rail for a bat?

A large catalogue might be made out. We had a multitude of social pleasures amongst ourselves. Despite the 'peelers', the laws, the customs, and traditions; despite the lack of a thousand and one things which seem necessary to other people's existence, we were happy mortals.

In the summer we had the wild fruits, the river, and the lough. We had an idea—probably left over from the tribal period of the stone age—that there were no property rights in turnips or sloes, haws or blackberries. We felt that the crab-apples were our gifts from Providence. Of course, if the owner of the land turned up, we scampered off.

There was no law to prevent us from enjoying a sunset, a cloud effect, or the wealth of golden sunshine. The wild flowers were ours, and we could look over the walls into the gardens of the more highly favoured. Besides, we had a garden of our own. It only measured 36 by 24 inches, but my mother grew nasturtiums, pansies, geraniums, and a currant bush in it. She used to say that in the growing of flowers love was as necessary as water. That seemed foolish to us. But somehow when she went away, flowers ceased to grow there. Something was missing; we could not tell what it was. Less and less grew in it every year, and finally it was swept away altogether.

III

The beginnings of routine began before I was ten. To be tied down to hours was to me like being put in a cage. Of course, selling papers isn't a job—it's a point of departure at which nobody ever intends to remain. I began there, but my first real job was gathering gooseberries. I had a weakness for them. When I got the job of gathering a small garden crop, I began to see visions and dream dreams.

The old gentleman who owned the garden took me out and gave me instruction. He hovered around all the forenoon. In the afternoon he had business elsewhere, and had to leave me. Before leaving, he told me that in his absence I was to whistle, and keep on whistling until he returned. This was something

21

not nominated in the bond, but I whistled and whistled until my mouth was sore. I stopped once just to see if anything would happen, and something did. A lady came out and took the old man's place. To have such solicitation and care literally showered on me in my first job had a wholesome moral effect. I whistled on and on with a conscience that would have served me well under other circumstances, if I could have kept it up.

The old man rewarded me for this by giving me a job in the harvest time. At least I looked upon it as a reward. I was one of four boys making straps with which to tie the bundles of corn. It was hard work to keep up with the reapers. In order to keep us at top speed, the old man had a pail of water at the other. If we kept up close he would send us when thirsty to the milk. If we lagged behind he would send us to the water.

At dinner time my gooseberry conscience collapsed! When no one was looking I changed the pails. I was foolish enough to let the other boys into the secret, with the result that they shamefully malingered and lagged behind. The milk pail was soon emptied. At the close of the day we sped off to the main road in a criminal state of mind.

Next morning he stood us up in a line like militiamen, and read out the sentence. Being a strict Presbyterian, he opened up the family Bible and in stentorian tones read: 'All liars shall have their place in the lake that burneth for ever and ever!' We resigned, under a cloud!

If I had been enmeshed in the toils of the law in my youth, my crime would have been committed to satisfy my hunger. There were rabbits, hares, and pheasants in plenty, and I knew where they were and

how to get them. Why did I not run the risk? In more highly civilised communities and in many savage tribes, the right to live is a distinct consciousness. Braver men and savages fight for it. Our mental attitude towards life was of such a character that the right to live had no standing whatever.

We had two alternatives to theft or violence, the poorhouse and degradation by begging. Death by starvation was preferable to the first, and theft was more honourable than the second. Antrim poorhouse was crowded to the doors, fifty years ago. Today, they are wondering what to do with it? There are no paupers. What has happened? A new democratic conscience overspreads the world. It has reached Antrim. Part of that conscience is the right to life. I can hardly say we were too cowardly to assert it in those days. We were bespunked, servile, and submissive to an invisible authority, which to us was both law and gospel. It wasn't a case of making the most of bad job. In our stupidity we never imagined it a bad job. Even if we had, we had no power to mend it. Our fathers having no property, had no votes. Nor would votes have helped the situation, for they would have been used for religious, and not for economic or political purposes.

IV

About the first of November, each year, there was a falling in attendance at the Sunday School of the Parish Church, and a corresponding increase in the Sunday School of the Methodists in the Kill Entry. Each year we were warned. Each year we turned a deaf ear to the warning. We were not deserters or 'turncoats'. Our annual lapse was not due to

24

disloyalty. The Methodists used to give a Christmas Soiree. Hot coffee and buns were served, with an address by an escaped missionary as a sort of spiritual salad. The Methodists knew all about our needs and capacities. They were generous to a fault, and we denizens of the alleys just took advantage of the buns they annually cast upon the turgid waters of the underworld.

About the first of January we slunk back again and rehabilitated ourselves. I presume we were catalogued in both organisatons as 'floating population'. But that hot coffee and the buns were worth all the disgrace they cost.

The Methodist watch-night service was of fascinating interest to me. It was a rather doleful, sombre occasion, but I liked such things. They appealed to the imagination. During the last half-hour of the year, the Methodists used to hold an evangelistic service at the gates of the Parish Church. It wasn't one of those 'weather permitting' affairs. It was held weather or no weather.

I think the leaders used to look upon us proletarians of the Parish Church as being as much in need of a 'sound' conversion as any of the old tatterdemalions who hung around the pubs. So they warned us in stentorian tones. I confess I liked this hell-fire admonition. It made me shiver, but it also reconciled me to the frosty mid-night air and the cold pavement under my bare feet. There was no levity. Those inclined to that sort of indulgence remained in the little chapel and sprinkled cayenne pepper in the hymn books to give the saints a sneeze on their return from the open-air meeting.

I remember one night being led by old 'Chisty' McDowell back to the chapel. He took my hand and held it all the way. I remember, too, what I was thinking about. I had an idea that he would get to heaven before I did. I imagined myself at the gate. If there was any fuss or hesitation on the part of the gate-keeper, I would send in for 'oul Chisty', and if he had any influence I knew he would use it on my behalf.

The closing sentences of the leader were solemn and sometimes terrifying. 'A few moments yet remain of the old year,' he would say. 'You have yet time. This voice may never again warn you on a watch-night. Let your sinful life pass away with the old year—it is going, going, going—it is gone!'

How terrible the sounds of the church bell as it clanged out the old year! How solemn the thoughts of the little crowd as it walked up the dark street to the chapel!

In order to enjoy this midnight meeting I had to have a special writ of indulgence from the chimney corner. All other nights the ringing of the curfew bell at 9 pm brought me home. There were a few other special permits. There were a few thrills of another kind. The McCormacks—a band of travelling players, came to our town once a year. They put up their theatre on the barrack square, and gave us a whole week's melodrama. The last time I enjoyed this beggar's Opera, I did so by virtue of the fact that I blew the bellows for Johnny Cooper, the nailer—twopence a day, for a week. I don't think the performances would have elevated a cow, but they thrilled us for the time being, and formed just one more gateway to the world that lay beyond—'over the hills and far away'.

There were other thrills. One of the great spiritual and intellectual treats of my youth was a lecture on the *Pilgrim's Progress* by a man who brought the pilgrim journey closely home to us by the aid of a magic lantern. I got more benefit from it than from all the sermons I ever heard. Most sermons were a pious bore to our dull intellects anyway. They were preached in a language we did not understand, and concerned themselves with themes utterly beyond our ken.

I do not believe that any community in the three kingdoms was ever so completely left to its own resources. 'Our betters' felt no responsibility toward us. If they had only known that they had the power to lift our somewhat sordid lives to a higher plane, they might have given us a little more of themselves. We had capacity for greater things. We could have been stimulated to greater intellectual effort, and it would have taken so little time or effort to do it.

> Who gives himself with his alms
> Gives three,
> Himself, his hungry brother,
> And me.

> Lowell

Chapter 2

THEMSELVES

I

It was the popular minister of an unpopular church (Unitarian) who used to give lectures on the history of Antrim. From him we learned that the great men of the past, whose names were connected with the old town, were, an archbishop, a great theologian, a learned professor, and a poet.

The archbishop couldn't help being born in Antrim, but in his autobiography he could avoid mentioning the fact—and did so. The learned professor extended the frontiers of the knowledge of his day. Throughout his long career he seems to have had an affectionate regard for his birthplace. The poet cut short what promised to be a brilliant career by drowning himself in the river that flows through the town. The theologian, having been chased out of England on theological grounds, took refuge with our people and preached with freedom in the Parish Church for some years.

But the men who were great townsmen in my youth are unknown to fame. Their names are not found in the pages of history. They are enrolled in the musty records of the churches and in the faded, worm-eaten books of the tax gatherers—and some of them can be found only in the latter.

John Conlon was the town Process Server—a minor court official whose duty it was to deliver

28

court summonses. The Conlons were our kind of folk. They lived in a four-roomed house on the front street, but despite the superior social status, we were the most intimate friends.

When John started off each morning with his bundle of trouble under his arm, all the neighbours looked his way. He was a model of neatness. He wore a tall hat, and by virtue of that we called him 'Mister'. The hat was always shiny—on the outward journey. His black cravat was neatly tied, his gray hair was parted at the back, and his whiskers were always neatly trimmed. He was rather short, but walked with a military stride, head well poised and his shoulders pressed back.

Few knew the secret of his scrupulously careful toilet. I did, because I knew Eliza, his wife. She was John's valet, housekeeper, and devoted wife. In John there was an aristocratic strain. Eliza was a proletarian. There were times when John returned from the work of the day with his beaver slightly tilted to one side, and his wellingtons got in each other's way. It was not a daily occurrence, but frequent enough to make it well known. On such occasions John talked as if he had just been lowered from the seats of the mighty into our midst at the bottom of the world. He would remind Eliza of the gulf that yawned between their social stations and suggest as he coughed and cleared his throat, that he had come down.

'Wasn't it nice ov ye, dear!' she would say, as she pulled off his wellingtons and made him comfortable in the corner. His language was always correct, his words chosen with care and discrimination. No magistrate that I knew had such a gift of fine language. John did not need to inform us of his superiority. We had a respect for him that bordered on reverence.

'Eliza, my dear,' he would say on the morning after the night before, 'I have a dim recollection of having used language in your presence last night that was unbecoming a gentleman. I offer you an unqualified apology, my dear!'

'God love ye, dear,' she would reply, 'shure I knew rightly it was because ye'd haad a haard day!'

'You must put it down to the inebrious influences of my legal vocation—I am a limb of the law—a lower limb.'

These exchanges were usually delivered as Eliza was putting the finishing touches to his cravat or brushing his frayed frock coat. No aristocrat was ever better groomed, no epicure ever had more attention paid to his table. The cottage was small, the floor was of mud, the stones around the wide, open hearth were whitewashed. The shelves of delft were neatly arranged. There was an air of scrupulous cleanliness such as was found in no other house in our immediate neighbourhood. After breakfast his tall hat and staff were handed to him, and with his leather case full of trouble he went off on his daily round.

'I need not tell you, Mr —— ,' John would say, as he entered a house with a summons, 'how embarrassing it is for me to enter your abode as a mere cog in the machinery of the law!'

'Don't mention it, Mister Conlon,' he would be told, 'shure it's yourself that's as welcome as th' flowers o' May! Sit down, sir!' No matter where he went, no matter how bitter the legal fight, his exquisite English, his gracious manner, his genuine sympathy, won him an instant welcome. Often the

30

welcome was washed down with something, and it was this something that tipped his high hat on the side of his head and released his pent up oratory on the road home.

John made a great impression upon me when I was quite a small boy. He was an aristocrat who belonged to us. He was a picturesque figure in our drab community, and we were very proud of him—especially as he sallied forth in the morning. And when he was ill and the neighbours were speculating on his status in the next world, I asked my mother who would brush his wonderful tall hat if he got there before Eliza.

'Well, dear,' she replied, 'in the next world John's hat'll be made of gray mist, an' won't need brushin'!'

But Mrs Mulholland smacked her thin lips and half in fun and wholly in firm conviction, said, if we had hats at all they'd have to be cast iron 'to stand the hate', which was a little hard on John, to say nothing of the rest of us—but she belonged to St Comgall's.

The absence of John made a big gap in our wee world. I remember the conflicting thoughts that surged through my childish mind when they told me that John had gone. I wondered whether, after all, those occasions when his hat just could not maintain its accustomed balance, would matter. My father was not quite orthodox, but in the course of time his opinion became for me a definite conviction.

'Shure God's a rale Gintleman,' he said, 'an'll luk afther our John, ay, He will that, just as shure as gun's iron!'

Sam Johnson baked bread for a living. His career was religious leadership. He was a philanthropist— in a quiet way. I knew two men who for many years

31

wore Sam's cast-off trousers. I saw these same garments in their third estate when they were worn by the boys in these households.

Sam was mortally afraid that any one should ever find out that he gave these things away. Despite the solemn promise he always received from recipients of his kindness, half the town knew all about his good deeds. When his beautiful daughter, Elizabeth, became old enough to keep the shop, she became his almoner. I was in that shop a few weeks ago—a younger daughter keeps it now—Sam and Elizabeth having gone long since to their reward. One thing I wanted to know—only one.

'Excuse me,' I said, 'for asking, but is that the same treacle box that was there when I was a boy.'

'Yes,' said Sam's daughter, 'the very same.'

Out of the storehouse of memory I brought them—Sam and Elizabeth. By the help of the imagination I placed them there, one at a time, with their hands on the lever, and beneath the opened half of a penny bap!

It was a doleful day for our poor neighbourhood when the Johnsons outgrew their small business and moved down into High Street!

In the old days, when Sam used to get his winter's supply of hay, we always helped to put it into the barn. What a joy to take a header into it, as it lay in the street! How we tumbled, cavorted, and played in it. He knew our limited resources, and invariably rejoiced at our simple, short-lived pleasures.

Sam Johnson was an Irishman in whom there was no guile. The shortcomings of our great men were as familiar to us as our old boots. We knew the weakness of his lordship. It was an open book to us. We knew the exploiters and the spoilers and profiteers of those days. Of Sam we knew only good Presbyterianism of the stricter sort had starched his spiritual column. His dignity could not be trifled with. He looked austere, but he had a great heart and his word was as good as his bond.

John Kirk, the grocer, was an outstanding figure. As a boy I looked upon him as our greatest political heretic. As I look back I am convinced that my judgement was based on the fact that he did his own thinking. Our point of view was ready-made. We inherited it. We hated things Irish and loved with a burning fanaticism things English—just because they were English. On politics and religion we had a closed mind. Those of us who had a chance to go to school were forced to study the history of England. We knew nothing about the history of Ireland. We didn't want to know. Ireland was Catholic. England was Protestant. Rags and dirt and ignorance was our common lot. Our representatives in Parliament were all of the landlord class. None of them were ever even remotely associated with movements for the uplift of the submerged. They didn't know we were sub-merged. We didn't know ourselves.

The finer aspect of this closed Ulster mind was that it had no selfish purpose or incentive. Few of us would have changed our mind for material gain.

In our part of the town only three houses subscribed for daily papers. Other papers came— weekly budgets of romance and adventure, but of the affairs of the world we knew nothing, cared nothing. Beaconsfield was our political demigod, Gladstone, Mephistopheles, and Parnell our Catiline. We never heard them, never saw them, never read anything they said. Our learned men knew, and that was sufficient for us.

33

We were taught to be content with that condition of life that God had mapped out for us. We were.

God, according to that principle or sophistry, had consigned us to ignorance and poverty out of which only a few ever escaped. When I dissociated that idea from God and righteousness, I remembered John Kirk, and was able in a measure to understand him. Whether I agreed with him or not, is another question. He had escaped from the fetters of ready-made opinions. He no longer wore the second-hand intellectual garments of his ancestors. He no longer bowed in the House of Rimmon.

II

Mr George Clarke, of 'The Steeple', was the magistrate I knew best. I knew the others by sight, but a regretable accident gave me a more intimate view of our senior interpreter and dispenser of the law.

The Steeple is Antrim's round tower, and is on the lawn of Mr Clarke's house, just beyond the railway station. There is a tradition that many centuries ago the round tower was in the centre of the town. Being the most perfect of all the round towers of Ireland, it would seem to men of ordinary mind that it should have remained a town possession.

Mr Clarke was a quiet, austere-looking man, who as he moved in and out of our streets, never seemed very familiar with anybody. His brother magistrate was Thomas Montgomery, whose reputation was of a similar character. Seldom did any of our townsmen attempt to express themselves in verse, but so pronounced was the neutrality of these worthies that

the following was passed from house to house when I
was a boy:

> George of the Steeple,
> And Tom of Burchill—
> They do little good,
> But they do little ill.

'Tom of Burchill' I knew by sight only. Mr Clarke
spoke to me once, but I made no reply. The
circumstances would not admit of an ordinary
exchange of civilities or an exchange of opinion.

In one of Mr Clarke's meadows there were a dozen
of the best sloe bushes in the parish. One afternoon I
was ensconced in one of them when a dog barked. I
looked around, and saw Mr Clarke approaching as if
he were in a hurry. I had business elsewhere at the
same moment. I was only twelve at the time, but
was more than a match at sprinting with a man over
sixty. He appealed to the dog, and the beast
responded. I had a start of about twenty yards. I left
Mr Clarke farther and farther behind, but the dog
was gaining on me every moment. A deep ditch or
'sheuch', as we used to call it, lay in my path to
freedom. On the other side was a fence. I cleared the
sheuch, but simultaneously as I grabbed the fence
the dog grabbed me. Happily for me the seat of my
trousers was rather baggy, and he got a mouthful of
that—held on to it, and still has it for aught I know
to the contrary, for I left it with him and escaped.
That was the nearest I ever came to social
intercourse with a fellow churchman and leading
light of my beloved town. The sloe bushes are still
there.

John Darragh was our village blacksmith. When I

used to stand dreaming at the smithy door, watching the flames spurt out of the live coals, old John had passed from the anvil to the bar. He was old and gray. He had only one eye, and he used that to run a public-house, leaving the smithy to his two sons.

John was a Catholic, but he didn't work much at it. But when he did favour St Comgall's with his swarthy presence, he wore a tall hat. He never wore it at funerals or celebrations. If he had we would have called him 'Mister'.

He was profoundly respected by our townspeople, especially by the boys. He had a fine group of gooseberry bushes, and could cover a wider range and a longer distance with that one eye of his than any other man could with a telescope.

There were not many outstanding figures in the town proper, but outside there were men who, in a measure, influenced its life and character. Mr Chaine was one of these. He owned the bleaching greens a few miles away, and employed a goodly number of men and women.

These were our supermen. When one of them was elected to Parliament we gathered around the big house to cheer, and perhaps get a mug of tea, and a bun, but we were socially connected to them with a rope of sand and industrially linked to their interests by a cash nexus. We drank wine from the common chalice at the Communion Table, but our communion began and ended there.

Johnston of Ballykillbeg was our great Orange leader, whose face was on our cups and saucers and plates. I deem it not an exaggeration to say that we worshipped him, in a way. Few of us around our quarter had ever seen him, but that may have been a factor in our worship. His name was on our lips, and

36

every time it was mentioned we felt like cheering. If we had spared a little of our zeal and emotion for New Testament characters, we might have been better off. That, of course, was foreign to our thought, and if it ever had occurred to us it would have been offset by the fiction that but for him we would have no New Testament at all.

We were being saved by him and his followers from something mysterious and dreadful. We never knew just what it was, and to have asked what we were being saved for would have been rank heresy—and we were all of one mind in congealed orthodoxy.

III

John Rae was a strange, erratic personality in those days. He was a Belfast lawyer of extraordinary ability. He was reported to be a terror to juries, and sometimes found himself in the county jail in consequence. Whenever he came to Antrim he was not only sure of an audience in the dingy court-house, but a gallery that followed him from the station.

A relation of ours got into trouble once, and Anna urged Jamie to betake himself to Belfast and see John Rae. He did, and John came. I was at the station with a hundred others—mostly boys and girls—when he arrived. He was a tall, broad-shouldered, gray-haired man. He had a very large forehead, and his great shock of hair was brushed back over his head. He wore a soft felt hat with very wide brim, and a huge military cape.

Wee Mr McTammany, who had charge of a solicitor's office in Antrim, met him and escorted him to the court-house. They walked in the middle of the road—the wee man almost trotting alongside the giant with the military stride.

Jim Suffern was charged with striking a blow that deprived Dan Heggarty of an eye. It was a fair day street brawl of the Orange-Fenian variety.

John Rae's opening address was spectacular, sensational, and characteristic.

'Gentlemen, shopkeepers, and others of the jury,' he said, laying his portmanteau on the table, 'Her Britannic Majesty's Orange-Fenian Attorney-General for Ulster presents his case and compliments to you!' Taking his nightshirt out and holding it up as he spoke, he continued: 'I have just emerged from the unhallowed precincts of the county jail, where, being the guest of Her Majesty, I was fed on the essence of shamrocks and sheep's trotters. You will observe I have come prepared for a journey to your Bridewell across the way if necessary!' His voice was loud, his gestures almost ridiculous. There were interruptions from the bench and scowls from the jury, but they only warmed him up.

The last witness was the complainant, Heggarty Rae reserved his heavy guns for him.

'You have confessed that on the day in question you had been drinking whisky. Now, Heggarty, tell the jury like an honest man whether you were overloaded or half-shot on that occasion!'

'Nayther,' said Heggarty.

'You hadn't lost your equilibrium?'

'I hadn't any to lose!'

'Thank you. That is quite frank.'

'What is it?' asked Heggarty.

'Since you had none, it is immaterial. How many men were in the shindy?'

'About a dozen.'

'All busy at the same time?'

'Yes.'

'The forces of Orangeism and Fenianism were equally divided, I presume?'

'Maybe.'

'Did you keep a record of the blows?'

'No.'

'Wasn't it possible?'

'No—not for me, anyway!'

'But you kept a record of one blow, didn't you?'

'Yes.'

'And that was the one you got on the eye?'

'Ay.'

'You kept no record of the one you gave?'

'No.'

'But you did give a few.'

'Yes.'

'Good ones?'

'I hope so.'

'But not quite so effective as this cardinal punch on your optic that was?'

'No.'

'You have been in McGuckin's public house since the fight?'

'Yes.'

'Is it true that every time you have been there you have carefully scrutinised the labels on the bottles?'

'Maybe.'

'And you have been a keen observer of things across the road—that is, you have tried to make a better use of one eye than you previously did of two?'

'I dunno.'

'But you never used to care what was on the labels before.'

39

'Oh, not particularly.'

'I will not intrude into your private affairs, Heggarty, but I believe you have really made closer observations in your own home than you did previously—is that not true?'

'Maybe.'

'And can you deny on oath that your wife hasn't more closely studied your face since the fight?'

'What has that to do with the case?' interrupted the prosecution.

'Just this,' said Rae, 'that a man's eye is not in his hinder parts but in his face, and the crux of the case is an eye. Come, Heggarty, on your oath, tell the jury whether or not your wife has, or has not, paid more attention to your face than before the fight?'

'Maybe.'

'I thought so. That sums up the case for the defence. Now, gentlemen and others of the jury, here is the kernel of the nut you have to crack. It is fair day in Antrim. Towards the close of the day, when tongues are loosened, and men hanker as only men of Antrim can hanker for something sensational with which to wind up a glorious day—what more natural than for the followers of Billy to express an ardent desire for a change of climate for His Holiness? What is there in our common, muddled existence more natural, than for admirers of His Holiness, of whom I am one, to resent this suggestion and desire his retention in the colder atmosphere of the Vatican? The complainant resented the suggestion that the change was either necessary or desirable. He did more: he rammed his resentment on somebody's facade with a punch. That was the curtain raiser to the Donnybrook Fair, described here in detail. Is anything more natural in Ireland than what

40

followed. Twenty-four fists flying in all directions. All at it all at one time, all bent on making an impression. No man armed with false knuckles or shillalahs. Just the common horny hands of toilers doing with their might what their hands found to do! Of course, there are the activities of cave men, but in this rumpus one cave man is singled out because he accomplished by accident what all of them desires to do deliberately. Gentlemen, an angel from heaven would have lost his mind trying to find out which of them planted the optic blow.

'But you have the evidence in front of you that the blow that put one light out, lit another and a brighter one. Heggarty lost an eye—he says he did—I haven't lifted that green patch to find out. I take his word for it. But note what happens. With one eye and a green curtain over the other window, he begins to use his mind. He observes things to which he had been as blind as a bat before. For the first time in this life he is awake to the beauty of nature. He knows now by his own careful observation that a hen sparrow is not a peacock, and all that is infinitesimal compared to the fac t that his wife begins to notice him. What a joy to a man who has become as common as old boots to be now the cynosure of his wife's admiring eyes! Why, gentlemen, there isn't a henpecked husband in the three kingdoms who wouldn't have one eye knocked out before bedtime if he could accomplish the same results! Heggarty, my boy, the Orange-Fenian Attorney-General for Ulster congratulates you and your wife and children to the third and fourth generation!

'Gentlemen, you will render a verdict on the evidence—the evidence of the complainant. He

41

struck the blow that started the fracas—the fracas that shut an eye opened his mind, and enlarged his miserable soul. If somebody had done that to me when I was his age, I would be now on the woolsack in the House of Lords, instead of swinging a convict's shirt in the fetid air of Antrim courthouse.'

The jury returned a verdict of 'Not Guilty'.

They have all, long since, passed into the great silence. Others have taken their places. John Rae went out by his own hand. The great and the near great, the wise and otherwise, the rich and the poor, all occupy about the same space in the ground, and their doings and sayings become more dim as the years go by.

Chapter 3

THE BOG-QUEEN'S FLITTIN'

I

In the long winter nights, when a turf fire burned brightly on the hearth and Jamie had put his shoemaker's bench aside for the day, we used to watch Anna's face with the keenest interest. We did not need to ask many questions—we could tell her moods as easily as we could tell the time by looking at the face of the clock. The mood we looked most eagerly for was the story-telling mood. Her stories shortened the night and gave a weird, mystic interest to a life that was not overladen with excitements. For the social hours of the evening a candle was lit and placed in the tin sconce that hung in her corner. Sometimes she read a story from a weekly newspaper—the only paper we ever saw in those days.

As we sat on the floor in front of the fire we were usually a sleepy lot, and as surely as Anna *read* a story, half of us children would stretch ourselves out on the floor and drop off to sleep. But when she *told* a story—whether it was a folk story she had heard in her youth or an original one spun out of the fabric of her own mind, we were wideawake from start to finish. Our interest was not held wholly by the story. She had a personality that gave the story charm and held us by its spell, helping us to forget many things of which the poor are acutely conscious down where we lived, at the bottom of the social world.

One never-to-be-forgotten night, when the snow lay deep on the streets and the wind howled in the alleys around us, Willie Withero, the stone-breaker, dropped in for a 'crack', and we moved closer together and made room for him. The kettle hung on the chain singing, and we were in high hopes that a cup of tea would be forthcoming, before we were sent off to bed. Withero's arrival enhanced the hope. He had a subtle vein of humour, and his quiet, humorous hints always produced results.

'I suppose,' said Withero, 'that ye boil the water for tomorrow's tay the night before, now, Anna?'

'Oh, no,' Anna said adroitly. 'Sufficient unto the day is the evil thereof, Willie; we have the tay the night before, and use our imaginations on the followin' mornin'!'

'Save us alive,' he said, 'isn't that a fine notion—and savin'?'

'Your mouth looks awful wathery, Willie,' Jamie chimed in—as anxious as Withero.

'Oh, ay,' Willie sighed. 'Me inside thinks me throat is cut, and that's no saucy feelin'!'

'Ye might as well make it, dear,' Jamie said, 'because as sure as gun's iron he'll palaver here all night and wind up by scalding his throat with that boiling wather!'

'It's the sinsible man ye are, Jamie,' was the stone-breaker's reply, 'an' that's no feerie story!'

The tea was made and shared around as we sat on the floor. Withero drank his in about three keys—mostly in G. Jamie added a few turfs to the fire. That was the invariable sign that as soon as Anna finished her tea he would insist good-naturedly on her telling a story.

44

Our minds became active at once. Should we beg for an old favourite, or take our chances on her own selection? Before we could give any expression to the fitful thoughts that flitted through our minds, Jamie had taken the initiative.

'I don't think Willie ever heard ye tell the "Queen's Flittin' "', Anna. Would ye just as soon tell that as anything else?'

This was an old favourite, and we backed up the suggestion as we settled ourselves in a tensely strung-up attitude of attention. There was a light in her large, dreamy eyes, her face was encased in a halo of white ruffled linen and an atmosphere of the tenderest mysticism filled us all with a sort of reverence and awe. In the telling of a story, she shortened the participles and added to her natural tone just the quaintest touch of an Irish brogue.

How real the wee people in that land of fairies were to us! Being highly sensitised and of clear, undimmed vision, she had missed most acutely that which she never possessed, and her story-telling made up for much in our lives and in her own. To doubt the reality of the world of fancy through which she led us, would have been to doubt our own existence.

II

'There was a king of Ulster a long time agone, and he was purty hard up for a queen. He was gey particular about beauty, and in them days there was a bad famine of good looks. One day he was walkin' along be the side of the lake, jist switherin' about nothin', when he seen a quare caper on the quiet wather by his side. A flock of wild geese dhrapped suddenly

46

into the lake with a splash and a yell like the laughter of childther. Jist as quick as ye could say "Jack Robinson" the white geese had turned into a wheen of the purtiest girls the king had ever set eyes on. He hid for a minute behind some bushes, jist to get a good look, and to do some more switherin'. As he did so he spied half a dozen bundles of girls's clothes.

' "Bedad, they're fairies," says he to himself. So just for divilment he grabbed one of the bundles and hid himself in a bunch of big ferns. After splashin' for a while, the girls came out. When one saw that her things were gone she cried and carried on terrible. Jist then a wee robin came hoppin' down the path, and a bright notion came into the girl's mind.

' "Robin, dear," says she, "if ye'll help me find me clothes, I'll put crumbs on me window-sill for ye for a year and a day!"

'The robin wagged his tail a bit, and then led her to the ferns where the king was hiding.

' "It's undacent," says she to the king, when she saw him, "to be holdin' a colleen's clothes like that." And with that she turned into a white goose.

' "Well," sayd he, "I'm King of Ulster, and I'm lookin' for a queen, and I thought maybe you'd be a cupid's guide-post and show me where to go."

' "Where have ye looked?" says she.

' "In the coorts of other kings and amongst the quality of the four provinces," says he.

' "Musha, that's no place for to be lookin' for a queen," says the goose-girl. "Go out into the counthry and see the girls that be creelin' turf in the bogs and the girls that dhrive home the cows. Shure beauty alone is but skin deep, and that's what we get in coorts and castles. But a useful life is a natural life, and a life lived with nature fills the heart with

47

music, and a heart that's full of music and love needs no paint on the face nor dhirty oil on fine clean hair."

' "Acushla, ye do be talkin' like a fairy!" says the king.

' "It's jist goose sinse," says she.

'Did she cackle or jist spake?' I ventured to inquire.

'Dhry up, ye wee gandther!' the stone-breaker said, as he spat into the fire and dunched me with his elbow.

Anna proceeded.

'Well, the king handed over the clothes, and turned his back while she put them on. When he turned around again, he was alone—except for the wee robin who sat on the lowest branch of an ash-tree singing a *Te Deum* over the good fortune of a year's provisions.

'Afther switherin' and sweatin' for a few days, the king dhressed himself as a boughal and——'

'What'a boughal?' I asked—keeping an eye on Withero's elbow.

'It's jist a bhoy that works (instead of playin' shinny) for a livin',' she said, and went on—'Dhressed as a boughal he thravelled over the five counties around Lough Neagh till he came to Antrim. Here he got shelter for the night in the abbey down near where the castle now is. Next mornin' he told the abbot, who could keep a secret, about his "quare" quest.

' "About a mile from the round tower," says the abbot, "ye will come across a peat bog. Ye might thry your luck there, and may the saints direct ye."

'With his pack on his back, his stick in his hand, and the luck of God in his heart, he dandthered off in the direction of the tower. Not far from the ould

48

steeple, he came to a bog where men were diggin' and girls were creelin' turf. The king asked a man on the road about the bog, and who its owner might be.

' "It's the turf bog of Dennis Mulvany," says the man, "and that's himself in his shirt sleeves."

' "The top of the mornin', Dennis," he said, as he looked over the hedge at the bogman.

' "Morra, bhoy," says Dennis.

' "Is it any work you would be havin' for a hard-workin' boughal?" asked the king.

' "Ay, work and plenty," replied the bogman, "but I don't pay gomerals to blether with the girls."

' "Ay," says the king, "but it doesn't do to be uncivil to the girls these days, Dennis."

' "Is it work or women ye're afther lookin' for?" says Dennis.

' "It's work," says the king.

'So Dennis gave the royal boughal a spade and put him to work. Past where the king was diggin' Nora O'Connor was creelin' the dry peat to a stack. She was the purtiest colleen in the whole glen. It was the blue eyes of her and the skin ye could look through, it was that fine and beautiful. No wondther at all at all that the king was struck speechless at the first sight of her. She would thrip so softly over the sod in her white, bare feet, singing an ould Irish song.

' "Ye've forgot to be diggin,'", she said once as she passed.

' "Oh, ay," says the king, "there's a kink in me power of remimbrance since I first laid eyes on ye."

' "Ye must have more thoughts than ye know what to do with," says she, laughin'.

' "Ye're a good guesser for a girl," says he.

' "Maybe ye'd sell me a farthin's worth of thim," says she.

' "I'll give ye a wheen for nothin' if ye'll linger a minute," says he.

' "It's not mesilf that would be mindin' at all, but Dennis," says Nora, with a knowin' smile.

' "Dhrap yer sheep's eyes on yer work, there!" roared Dennis across the bog; and Nora thripped off with her creel.

'At dinner time the king let on that he had nothin' to eat at all, and of course he told the fair Nora. She shared her dinner with him. In matters of the heart he made hay while the sun of opportunity was shinin'.

' "Perhaps," says he, "a kind-hearted colleen like yourself could tell a poor boughal where to find lodgin' and food with dacent people.?"

' "I'll ax me father," says she.

' "I'll go down with ye and hear what he says," he answered.

'And home to the cabin be the side of the woods they went as the shadows began to fall.

'As they came to the round tower they lingered awhile, just switherin' and wondtherin' who built it, and why and for what earthly use. As they stood for a minute, Nora put her beautiful white hand on one of the ould stones a wee bit higher nor her head, and jist as quick as ye could wink yer eye the king took his cap in his hand and clapped it over the hand.

' "Behave!" says Nora, as she quickly dropped her hand.

' "A million pardons!" says the king. "I thought it was a butterfly."

' "If yer heart's as fine as yer complimints, I hope ye'll get lodgin' at our cabin," she said, as she turned away her head for the blushes.

'As they went along, the king sort o' shyly took

hold of her hand jist to make sure she wasn't a fairy.

'There was quite a palaver in the cabin that night. The old man gloured and the old woman axed questions, and Nora, with her arms akimbo, looked on and hoped.

' "Who's yer father?" axed Phelim O'Connor.

' "Me father's dead," says he, "but he was a man of an ancient line, one of whom was Durtracta, the disciple of St Patrick, who built the abbey of Antrim."

' "A terrible *descint* from that to *this*!" says Mrs O'Connor, pointin' to the boughal.

' "Ay, thrue for you, mother," says he; "but it's mesilf that's goin' to regain lost fortunes, with the help of God."

' "He's a wondtherful worker," sayd Nora—God forgive her!

' "Purty good testimony, me girl," says her father, "if ye wor in the witness-box, which ye don't happen to be at this moment."

' "For why should ye pour cold wather on the warm heart of youth?" says she, with a toss of her purty head.

' "Ye were sint out to work in the bogs, me girl—not to gather human mushrooms," said Mistress O'Connor.

'Well, they paveed and palavered one at a time, and all of thim at once, until at last the fracas ended by givin' the boughal his supper and a place in the corner among the peat coom as a bed for the night.

'The kind was happy. He dhramed the most beautiful dhrames of purty colleens and fairies and earthly paradises in which Nora moved about as a queen.

'Nixt mornin' Nora and the strange boughal went

51

off again to the bogs, but durin' the day a terrible mishap befell the king.

' "Me bhoy," says Dennis, when he caught him throwin' kisses afther Nora, "ye'd betther go for a sodger or a king or somethin', for ye couldn't earn pirta peelin's at diggin' turf. Ye do nothin' from mornin' till night but glour at the girls, and all that's to be done in that direction I'm purty well inclined to do myself."

'So he ordthered the king out of the bog; but the king wouldn't budge an inch until ould Dennis hit him a whack with his shillalah. The king paid him back with more interest than was laygal, and would surely have kilt ould Dennis entirely but for the intherference of Nora.

'That night he waited for the colleen, and they walked home the longest way around. As they went through the woods, hand in hand, talkin' much and sayin' little, they heard a noise—"rat-tap, rat-tap!"

' "That's the Leprauchan," says the king.

' "We'll ax for three wishes," says Nora, laughin'.

' "Is that you, Misther Leprauchan?" shouted the king.

' "Yis," says the quare voice of the fairy shoemaker.

' "We want our three wishes," says the king.

' "Out wid thim," says he, "for I'm gey busy mendin' boots for the fairy ball that's to be given in the round tower the night."

'For a minute the young people stood scratching their heads and puzzlin' their minds over wishes. Then the king spoke.

' "A king for a husband for this colleen!" says he.

'Nora laughed.

' "Hurry up!" says the Leprauchan.

' "A coach and four white horses for the wedding," says Nora, clappin' her hands in glee.

' "And a fairy friend for time of throuble," says the king, and the Leprauchan wint on with his work.

' "Why didn't ye ax for somethin' for yourself?" Nora said, as they meandered home.

' "Because," says he, "me name's already in his book."

' "What did ye ax for?"

' "Somethin' he couldn't give to two people!"

' "And what may that be?"

' "The most beautiful colleen in the world."

' "Ah, shure, ye're jist bletherin', for they do be sayin' that the king himself is thravellin' the world over in search of that same colleen."

"Ay, I've heard that same; but the Leprauchan says that only the king and meself have the ghost of a chance—and between you and me, I think I'll bate him!" '

III

'At the O'Connor cabin that night the king was full of blarney. Around the peat fire he told tales of fairyland. He reeled off long poems of love and romance. He sung the songs of Carolin and the bards of long ago. He paveed around the old folks and told of the wondtherful friends he had at the court of the king. He axed them for Nora, and Nora for herself, and every one of the three of them said, "Yes," but the night is the time for switherin', and Mistress O'Connor had worn her thinkin' cap.

'At breakfast she said: "Look here, me boughal, is it Nora ye would be afther marryin'?"

' "Ay," says he; "ye're a good guesser to know nothin'—it is that."

' "Well, thin," says she, "before we consint ye'll have to have money enough to buy an ass and a cyart and sell yer own thurf in the town of Anthrim."

' "It's a bargain," sayd he.

'Ould Phelim wanted to take a hand in the bargainin', but he was tired and all throughother, and just yawned and stretched himself, and, with his mouth as wide open as a coal-scuttle, said: "Ochanee-o-ho-him-ho-harry! If I was a maid I would niver marry."

'Nixt day the king became bould. He wint off with Nora in the mornin', but instead of goin' to the bogs they wint off to the Antrim fair, where he bought an ould cuddy and cyart.

'Afther cavortin' around for a while, they got into their cyart, and sittin' purty close tigither they druv home.

'As they passed ould Mulvany's bog, the king stood up, and called over the hedge to Dennis:

' "Ho, there, Mulvany, ye poltroon! Come over here till I give ye a taste of me tongue!"

'Dennis, with clenched fists and glarin' eyes, came and looked at the pair in the cyart. He stood for a minute in silent eloquince. Thin says he: "Ye decavin' baby thief—ye sacriligious, dundther-headed haythen! May the spotted favor split ye in four halves!"

' "Put a turf in that torn pocket of a mouth of yours, me bhoy, while I dhrive some sinse through yer copper cranium," says the king.

'Dennis scowled: Nora laughed.

' "Now, ye divil," says the king, "how much will ye take for yer bog?"

' "Ye uncivilised, playbayian baste!" says Mulvany, "ye haven't enough money to buy a feather out of a sparrow's tail."

'The king slipped his hand into a secret pocket and took out a warrant signed by the king. He showed it to Dennis. It was for a big sum of money.

' "Now, Mulvany, ye imp of Satan," says he, "go into Anthrim and get the Scribes and Pharisees to make out a lagal thransfer of your ould bog to me, and I'll hand ye the money!"

' "Ye're the broth of a bhoy," says Dennis.

' "Ay, and me mither niver sould soup, naither," says the king, as he hit the ould cuddy on the harness and jogged on toward the home of the O'Connors.

'That night, ould Phelim and his wife, seein' as how the strange boughal had the luck of God in his pocket as well as in his heart, were uncommon kind to him.

' "Ye would like, maybe, to sit by the fire tonight with the colleen," says Phelim.

' "It's a mind-reader ye are, Phelim," says the king.

' "We're goin' right off to lave ye," says Mistress O'Connor.

' "The sooner the betther," says he.

'The lovers put on extra turf and sat in the chimney corner tellin' feerie stories and readin' fortunes in each other's hands. They looked into each other's eyes and every one of the two of them confessed that it was like peepin' into heaven through a slit in the sky, or lookin' at the world through a stained-glass window. They did that. They played the old-fashioned game of measurin' each other's lips, but the noise nearly woke up ould

55

Misthress O'Connor, and they just bethought themselves and behaved quietly.

'But the fairies heard them, and there was the sound of wings—maybe of angels, who knows? There was the scint of bog-mint and violets and the sweet singin' of birds that forgot to be sleepin', and if ould Mulvany had known what has happening he'd shurely have forgot to be sleepin' too.

'When the boughal tore himself away from Nora, and Nora away from him, there was a moistenin' of eyes with the dew of the heart, and a tug at the heart-strings that made strange sounds. As they went to sleep, it was Cleena herself, the fairy queen from far-off Munster, who closed their eye-lids and held them down fast till they passed through the gates into the land of dhreams!'

IV

'As they sat at their stirabout and butthermilk nixt mornin', the boughal raised his bowl, and, says he:

> "In the essince of shamrocks
> I dhrink to the health
> Of the house of O'Connor!"

'Then he spake of his plans for a journey across Lough Neagh. He would be away some days, but on his return he would bring the most beautiful colleen in the world a message from the king himself. He would that.

'So with this stick in his hand and his bundle on his back, he started on his journey. Nora wint with him as far as the bridge across the Six-Mile-Water.

There, with an ache in her heart, and a quiver on her rose-red lips, she gave him her blessin' and let him go. As he wint through the wood between the river and the lough, he was singin'; for his heart was light with love, and be the help of the fairies his quare quest had been crowned with success.

'One mornin', as Nora was dhrawin' water from the well, she heard the clatther of horses' feet. Lookin' toward the road, she saw four white horses, and behind them a strange kind of carriage, and in the carriage sat the idol of her heart, her boughal, dressed jist as he wint away. On the seat in front sat two warrior-like men in doublet and hose and hats with tall red plumes.

' "It's as the Leprauchan said! God save us alive!" says she, as she ran out to embrace her bhoy.

' "It's the king's own carriage, Mavourneen," says he, "and it's married ye are to be in his castle this day."

' "And it's laving us behind ye would be?" says Mistress O'Connor.

' "Not at all, not at all," says the king. "Jump in mother! Come on, Phelim, me bhoy! Step lively, for we're off to spend the day with royalty, even though we be hung, drawn, and quarthered tomorrow!"

'So they clambered into the royal cyart just as they were, without boots or socks or coverin' of any kind for their heads. The boughal and Nora sat side be side and cavorted and capered all the way there. And they dhrove past Mulvany's bog that was.

' "This bog," says he, "is where Phelim O'Connor cuts turf for the king hereafter."

'Ould Phelim laughed, but Misthress O'Connor looked glum.

' "It's too uncanny to last, Phelim," says she;

"it's dhramin' we are and may God prevint us from wakin' up in Purgatory or jail, or the poorhouse!"

'When they had be dhrivin' half a day, the king ordhered the men to stop the carriage. He unlocked a wee secret door, and brought out a table and things to ate and dhrink. He laid the table with his own hands—Nora helpin', of course—and it was on the side of the road undther a sacred ash that they ate. He had butther-milk to dhrink the king's health in, but Phelim it was who said, "For playbayins like us the essince of shamrocks is good enough, me bhoy; but whin ye dhrink the health of a king, ye should do it with the kind of dhrink that goes down yer throat like a torch-light procession and a brass band."

'The king shtripped a suspicious lookin' bottle of its straw jacket and gave Phelim a cup. The ould man smacked his lips and looked wicked in the eyes.

' "Saints alive!" says Phelim, whin he could spake, "I'm after breakin' a commandmint!"

' "What is it?"

' "I'm covetin', agra."

' "Covetin' what?"

' "A giraffe its long neck, so that I could feel the sup as it flowed for a mile into my interior economy."

'In the twilight they arrived at the castle gates.

' "Glory be!" says Misthress O'Connor; "is it hung or thransported ye'd be gettin' us this day—to be threspassin' on the king's domain'?"

' "Whisht!" says Nora, "it's himself has axed us!"

' "It's me heart that's hungerin' for boots," says Phelim.

' "Me, too," says Nora.

' "Niver mind," says the husband that was to be. "If it'll make ye more comfortable I'll take mine off."

'As a gaily dhressed man came out to meet him,

Phelim and his wife dhropped on their knees.

' "Get up," says the king. "That isn't himself—it's the butler."

'Phelim gave the man a look that would wither the laves on a tree. "Ye uncivil galoot!" says he, "for why do ye be lettin' a dacint man be makin' a fool of himself?"

'When the man took them within, the poor craithers slid along on the smooth boards and saft rugs—the feelin' was good to the feet. They touched the purty things in the hall and gloured around in wondthermint.

' "Phelim, darlin', I think we're bewitched," says the wife.

' "I'm thinkin' we're blinked," says he.

'Nora was handed over to half a dozen ladies. They took her to a bath and thin to a wardrobe, and thin—of coorse—to a lookin'-glass.

' "It's jist sleepin' I am, " says she, "for there's a crown on me head, and you've dhressed me up as a queen!"

' "Is there anything yer heart could wish?" says one.

' "Oh, ay, deed there is now. Let me mother come here as soon as the laws of commotion will let her."

'Thin in came her boughal, and he was royally robed, with a crown on his head!

' "It's foolin' the world ye are!" says Nora.

'It was himself that laughed as he took her in his arms and let out the secret that he wasn't a boughal at all, but jist lettin' on. And they laughed as they held on to each other, and the crowns did topple here and there in an ungracious and unbecomin' way on their heads—and they throd on the tails of each other's clothes and slithered and slid till the

Dowager Duchess O'Connor came in with her nose in the air like a paycock.

' "Yer kingdoms are fallin' off yer heads," says she, as she fixed the crowns shtraight.

' "How did *you* find out?" says the king.

' "I took the colleen that washed me feet," says she, "and put her in a corner with me fist close to her nose, till she towld me who ye were, and savin' yer prisince I didn't have to detain her long!"

' "Where's me father?" says Nora.

' "Lost in the shuffle," says the Dowager Duchess. "I haven't laid eyes on him since he was on his marrow-bones before the butler."

'Poor Phelim at this time was jist meanderin' around like a lost child. Nora sent her mother to look for him.

' "O'Conor," says she, whin she found him, "how would I look on a load of turf with yoursilf as dhriver now?"

' "I remimber how ye did look whin I took ye from yer father's bog."

' "Dhry up! says she, "and put on a few manners, even if they will become ye."

'Jist than a man took Phelim away and overhauled him. Later, when he appeared like a corpse dhressed for the funeral, the guests gathered for the weddin'. There were lords and ladies, jooks and jookesses. There were cyart-loads of flowers and prisints galore. Jist as the archbishop was puttin' his robes on, Nora took the king aside to a quiet place and told him of a fear in her heart.

' "Oh, Misther King," says she, "the wee people of the glen do say that kings do sometimes git tired of their queens. I've been out in yer garden, and undther a yew-tree I did hear a green linnet singin', and the song he sung was this:

> ' "Ye're sailin' in unknown seas, colleen,
> And the rocks are many ahead;
> Ye need some help at the hilm, colleen,
> To clear yer heart of its dread.

So I did ax for a pilot, and the linnet was a fairy prince, and told me what to do."

' "And what did he tell ye to do, me queen?" says the king kindly.

' "I am to ax ye for a marriage conthract, and in it ye are to promise that if iver ye get tired of Nora O'Connor, ye will give her whatsoiver she desires that three asses can dhraw away." '

Here the story ended for the night. Jamie was nodding. Withero was getting fidgety; the candle had burned low in the sconce, and the fire needed Jamie's reluctant attention.

'Did his nibs sign up, Anna?' asked Withero.

'Come in to-morra night, Willie, and find out,' she answered.

Chapter 4

A KING'S HONOUR AND A QUEEN'S WIT

I

Next night we were gathered around the fire again. Withero was in his place. The kettle was on the chain, but we were warned that no hints would disturb it until the story had been finished.

'That's for me, I suppose,' said the stone-breaker; 'but if the Tower of Siloam falls I won't be the only cuprit in need of a pine suit.'

'The king had the conthract made jist as Nora wanted it,' Anna proceeded. 'The ceremoney took place, and thin the guests wint away. Ould Phelim and his wife were dhriven back home. Misthress O'Connor, of coorse, took home her new finery and wore it on market days. It was as good as a show to see her—and admission was free. It took her some time to git used to it. Phelim said the new things hurt him, so he wore the things that didn't. At first he couldn't stand the high-falutin' lingo of his wife. "Ivery time she opens her mouth," he said, "she puts her foot in it, and bedad! the worst of it is that I want to stick mine in too!" Vanity is short lived and dies hard, but time helps out a good dale. In time her nose came down out of the air, and Phelim was more contint.

'Queen Nora grew in sinse and good judgmint. She didn't forgit the bogs nor the bog people. She was loved and honoured be high and low. Two purty childther came, one afther another, and while her husband ruled Ulster, she ruled her household—but it's recorded that while she had wisdom enough and a little to spare, her husband hadn't quite enough. When there's any wisdom around, people soon find it out, for whether we live on pirtas and butthermilk or on fine bread and nightingales' tongues, we need wisdom, and wisdom is the mother of judgmint, and that's what a king man needs.

'The king got in the habit of axin' Nora for her advice in matthers of state. So did the king's counsellors. So did all sorts of folks with all sorts of throubles. None of thim axed in vain. She wasn't consated about it, nayther. Whin great men were lookin' for wives, the king always told them to go to the bogs, "for there," says he, "is where the queen came from, and there isn't anything jist as nice on the face of the earth as she is!" Which reminds me of the verse:

'Oh, Willie, honey, but love is bonny
A wee while, and when it's new;
But when it's old, oh! it grows quite cold,
And it fades away like the mornin' dew!

'As the years went by, the queen seemed to get more wisdom, and the king more and more depinded upon her. Thin love became more and more common, and as it did he axed her less and less. Sometimes he got a bit jealous, and at times angry, just because in matters requirin' wisdom she was queen and king too.

'One day a test of judgmint came along. An ould man had a foal. In the same field there was an ould

63

garron. Quare enough, the foal took an uncommon likin' to him that wasn't its mother. The foal grazed with him, played with him, stayed with him. Ivery day it was the same. If it was bate away it came right back. This looked quare to everybody in gineral, and to the man who owned the garron in particular. It gave him a quare notion.

'The owner of the garron claimed the foal.

' "For why do ye claim the foal of me mare?" says the mare's owner, "and more betoken . . ."

' "What a fool ye must be to think that a horse which is a garron could ayther be father or mother to a foal!"

' "The foal stays with the garron," says he.

' "The moon stays in the heavens," says the other, "but that dizint prove that it's made of green cheese."

'But the man who owned the garron stuck to the foal, and the man who owned the mare took the matther to the judge, and from the judge to the king. The king was puzzled, but he didn't like to ax the queen. So he said: "Be the instinct of the foal," says he, "we will decide the owner. Put the mare at one end of the field, and the garron at the other, and to whomsoiniver the foal goes, will be the owner be orther of the king."

'The queen had come in, unbeknownst to the king, and had heard the contintion. Whin the men wint out, she laughed like a girl, and says she: "Your majesty," says she, "the most ignorant peasant in Ulster is wise enough to know that a garron can be nayther father nor mother to a foal. It's not be the instinct of a silly foal, but be the instinct of raison and justice that the case must be decided."

' "I forbid ye to meddle in state affairs," says he.

64

"There's only one authority here—and I'm him."

' "To have little wisdom yerself is bad," says she, "but to think that because ye haven't, nobody else has, is worse."

'The king left the hall, in pure madness, sayin' as he wint, "If ye iver interfere in my judgmint again, I'll sind ye back to the bogs from whince ye came!"

' "Well, dear," was her partin', "it's better to be a small frog in a big puddle than a big frog in a wee puddle, in which he has to stand on his head to get a dhrink!"

'Nixt day, the mis-trial of bad sinse came off. The mare and the garron were put at different ends of the field, and the wee foal was placed in the middle. In the time it takes to wink yer eye the foal galloped over to the ould garron, and be the foolish act became the property of the garron's owner. The king was there, and well pleased with himself—so was the foal's owner.

' "If that gomeral wasn't the king," said the owner of the mare, "he'd be a hearse dhriver or an undthershtudy to a lamplighter."

'One day the queen was out walking with her childther. As they wint along the road a man came along. As he came close to the queen, he took his cap off his head, and, holdin' it in one hand, he scratched his head with the other.

' "I'm the man who owns the mare, Your Majesty," says he. "May I ax ye a question?"

'The queen smiled, and said, "Yes."

' "What would Yer Majesty do if ye were in my place?"

' "I would consult the fairies," says she.

' "For why didn't yer husband do that same, God save us alive?"

65

'The queen laughed, and the man laughed too.

' "Listen, good man," says she. "Go down by the river tomorrow, take a fishin' rod, and when ye see the king comin' do ye turn around and be fishin' on dhry land."

'She towld him what the king was likely to say, and what he should answer back. The man wint away well pleased with what he thought might be an alley out of the main street of his throuble.

'Nixt day, as the king went down along the river bank to fish, he saw a man fishin' on the dhry land.

' "Why do ye be fishin' on the dhry land?" he axed the man. "Don't ye know it's foolish?"

' "It's no more foolish, Yer Majesty, than to believe that an ould garron can ayther be father or mother to a foal!"

'The king had the man put in irons for tellin' the truth, and himself it was that wint home in a towerin' tanthrum.

' "Tell the queen," says he to one of his ginerals, "to pack up her thraps and go back home to the bogs. I know that polthroon got his wisdom from her, and it's undignified to have any woman dictatin' to a king. That's me ordther—go and execute it, and ax me no questions!"

II

'The word that the queen was goin' spread like the maisles. The household was in tears. The ginerals hung their heads. The king hid himself, and well he might, the shtookawn.

'To the gineral who was to execute the ordther the queen showed the marriage contract, and axed him if he would be so kind as to execute that too.

' "I don't know, Yer Majesty."

' "In the case ye'll be quite at home here," says the queen.

' "I mean——"

' "It's meself knows what ye mean—there's no call for palaver."

' "What would Yer Majesty like put in the cyarts?" he asked.

'The queen swithered for a minute. "Deed," says she, "that taxes me own wisdom. I must swither over it."

'She wint into the garden, and, sittin' be the big yew-tree, she heard the linnet sing.

' "Oh, Prince of Fairyland," she said, "oh, greatest comforter in *Fir Nan Og*, do give me wisdom in this hour of sore trouble."

' "Ye've been unmindful of your fairy friends," says the linnet, "and now when in throuble you must have a test put to yer faith. Ye'll be given wisdom be the minit. Aych minit will bear on its back its own burden. Ye must live a minit at a time!"

'The queen came out of the garden and began to pass through her sore thrial—a minute at a time.

' "I'll be afther loadin' the cyarts, Gineral,' she said.

'The first cyart came to the door, and packin' began. Four dogs, three cats, a pet lamb, a parrot, a pet rabbit, and a canary. The second cyart came and was filled with toys, books, pictures, clothes, and the two childther.

' "Yer Majesty wouldn't be afther takin' away the heir to the throne?" says the gineral.

' "Ay, Sir Knight," says she. "Her Majesty may carry off the throne itself if she's given wisdom and stringth."

' "Saints in glory!" says he, "what would ye do with the throne?"

' "Sit on it in the bogs," says she, "and write sonnets to the moon."

' "Wouldn't that be a quare place for a throne now?"

' "Gineral," says the queen, "whatsoiniver a queen sits down on is a throne—whether it's a stool or mossy bank or a gilded box of a chair that niver sees the daylight."

'The queen jist palavered with the gineral while she was waiting for the nixt minute's wisdom. It seemed a year in comin'. Whin it arrived she knowed what to do, she did that.

' "Go ax His Majesty to pray God for enough of the instinct of an Irish gintleman to come down here and say good-bye to his wife and wains. Tell him his wife has only love in her heart—jist mixed wit a bit of throuble, of course—but that if he'll jist be a lover once again for five minutes and a father for one, he can believe not alone that a garron can be a mother to a foal, but that he can be a mother to the king himself, or of a white elephant or he did in the long ago, he can believe if he takes that a banty hen can lay swan's eggs, and out of thim hatch a flock of nice big whales. He can that. One word more. Gineral. If ye plaze, don't let a human soul be in sight if he comes to say good-bye—it's undignified for a king to let his lip thrimble or to have a dhrop of heart-dew on his eyelash. A wink's as good as a nod to a blind horse—ye understand?"

'The gineral wint to find the king, and the queen wint to spake comfort to the childther, who were whimperin' in the cyart. A dhriver had been provided for aych cyart. She sint two of thim off with the first two cyarts.

68

' "Go on down the road," says she, "and keep dhrivin' till I overtake ye.'

The dhriver of her own cyart she sent away, and in the courtyard she stood beside her cyart. As she stood she prayed for superhuman stringth for what her mind was set on. She knowed what to do, and aych minute brought more power. She was dhressed as a colleen of the bogs again, and niver in all her life had she looked so purty, so pure, so queenly.

'Down came the king.

'He was thryin' mighty hard to look unconcerned, but sure enough there was a thrimble of the lip and gawky awkwardniss that towld Nora how the land was lyin'.

' "Is the word of a gintleman good, bad, or indifferent?" says she.

' "It's good," says he.

' "I can have what I can take away in three cyarts?"

' "Ye can."

'She breathed a prayer, gathered all her strength, and, grippin' the king by the two legs, she dumped him into the cyart, and, as quick as lightnin', jumped in on top of him, gathered up the reins, hit the ass on the behind end, and off she wint.

' "Hould on!" says the king.

' "Hould on nothin'," says she. "I've got me flittin' and I'm off home to the bogs." '

'What did the gomeral do?' asked Withero.

'Well, Willie, he came to his sinses. The load on his stomach sort o' made him think—men bewhiles do think whin pressure is on thim.'

'Ay, with that kind o' pressure any man would think.'

'Well,' she continued, 'just like a woman whin her

hat isn't on shtraight, he says: "Is anybody lookin'?" says he.

' "No," says Nora.

' "Let me up," says he.

' "Are ye mine?" says she.

' "Yis," says he, "but ye've broken the conthract."

' "How's that?" says Nora.

' "Ye've taken four asses instead of three."

' "Oh, no, dear, ye're mistaken—it's only three asses: the other is an Ulster mule." '

● ● ●

The kettle came off the chain and we had the usual cup of tea all round. As we went off to bed we left Withero and Jamie in a heated discussion with Anna on the comparative amount of gumption in the possession of men and women.

Chapter 5

A CORNER IN LARKS

I

Michael was the niggard of our gang. From long experience we had learned to quicken our sensibilities when negotiating a trade of dicker with him. He had a soft, naive way of extending courtesies with invisible strings attached. Only one man in the glens of Antrim had ever gotten the better of a bargain with him. From this Shylock of Ballymena, Michael once purchased a parrot. The bird talked on the 12 November—fair day—but for some unknown reason never spoke again. Michael made the journey to Ballymena and protested vigorously.

'Michael me bhoy,' said the birdseller, as he tapped Michael's low brow in a familiar and friendly manner, 'I know'd when I sold Poll that he had a kink in his power of rememberin' words, but me broth of a bhoy, I also know'd piradventure without a moiety of a doubt that he was what no other man, woman, or chile was, or ever has been in yer measly wee town ov Antrim.'

'An' what might that be?' asked Michael.

'A devil ov a thinker, me bhoy!'

Antrim paid dearly for that Ballymena parrot. The story of the larks is only one item in the account.

We had just emerged out of the old swimming hole in the mill race one day, when Michael said in a casual kind of way:

'Yer oul' man's fond o' larks, isn't he?'

'Ay,' I replied, with chattering teeth, 'how did you know?'

'I guessed,' said Michael.

'Yer a purty good guesser to know nothin', said I.

'I know more'n yer think fur.'

'Wud ye let on t' me?'

'I know where there's a nest of larks.'

'Honest?'

'Ay.'

'How much for the whole nest?' I asked.

'I have half a dozen people figurin' on thim, but since I know ye're purty anxious, I'll make a special price!'

'Before ye drap down in price too suddenly, Michael—I—I—want to say'—I could see a sneer curl on Michael's big lips—'I jist want to say,' says I, 'that th' oul' man isn't so keen on larks this sayson!'

'No?' said Michael, as he sniffed the air in cold disdain.

'No,' said I demurely, 'a good cock thrush would jist about hit 'im right.'

Michael surveyed me with a look of withering scorn as he drawled out sarcastically—'Maybe a nice singing cuckoo would about shuit his paltry mind!'

Of course I wanted the larks. I wanted them as desperately as Michael wanted to sell them. It was a question of cost. Could I muster the price? Could I shave his demands down to my meagre resources?

'Come on!' I said abruptly, and as seriously as I could, 'Let's get down to business. What's th' lowest price ye'll take fur them larks?'

'Now, seeing it's you,' he began.

'Never mind s-e-e-i-n-g i-t-s m-e! seeing it's the larks, how much are they worth?' I insisted.

'What they're worth, an' what I'm axin', said he,
''as as much conniction as Ayster an' Christmas, but
if ye'll kape yer oul' shirt on awhile, I'll give ye the
surprise ov yer life—I will that!'

'Ye'll be selling them below cost, I'll bate, eh,
Michael?'

'Worse, me bhoy, worse nor that. I'll be making ye
a prisint ov thim, charging ye but fourpence for th'
time I've wasted an' th' moral shtrain on me narvous
system.'

'It's dhirt chape, Michael,' says I, 'but I'm sore
consarned about yer narves. Antrim could poorly
afford t' lose sich a lark merchant!' Michael
explained that in business he was a dual personality—one of him always undercharging, and the
other the reverse. Some of the compromise must
have been struck, for Michael is now an old
man—wealthy, and showing no sign whatever of the
terrible strain of those earlier years.

I inquired about terms, whether a penny a week
would be acceptable? I offered a mortgage on several
bird cages, and was willing to bind myself by any
number or style of oath necessary to fit the case.
Michael was obdurate. 'That's jist blether,' he said.
'Money talks!'

'Michael,' says I, 'it's a bargain! Whin can I take
thim?'

'Whin can ye be afther paying something?'

'Jist as soon as I'm afther finding out they're not
sparrows.'

'I don't think ye've got sinse enough,' said
Micheal, 'to tell the difference betwixt a paycock and
a cock robin!'

'Come on, now, ye haythin baste,' said I, 'be
dacent, and if ye can't be dacent, be as dacent as ye

73

can, and tell me when I can get thim.' Michael folded his arms and looked at me with an air of pity. I felt as if he could see down into the depths of my empty pockets.

'There is, at least, a baker's dozen o' people that wants them larks,' he said slowly, 'an' I think I'll close up wid one ov them,' and with that he walked off and left me.

That night I went over the matter with my father. He knew Michael better than I did, and advised me accordingly. 'Don't pay a ha'penny down till ye see th' birds,' he said.

II

Next morning I was about early and watching for Michael. No devotee ever hung around the shrine of a saint with more enthusiasm—nor did Jacob possess more intense desire when he took a fall out of the angel, than I possessed that morning at the mouth of the alley as I awaited the appearance of the lark man. Finally he emerged—I followed a furlong or two behind. Then accidentally I overtook him. He was headed for Gowdy's meadow.

'Where are ye fur?' he asked, as I pretended to pass him.

'Jist for a dandther!' I replied.

'I'm off fur a look at the larks,' he ventured, in a casual way. 'Wud ye like t' g'long?' I told him I was rather busy, but I thought I could spare the time. We turned down Mill Row and went along the bank of the river, past the paper mill to Gowdy's meadow. As we went along, he endeavoured to impress me that he possessed unerring judgement in larks. His talk was wondrously wise—full of big words and veiled allusions.

'Ye could make a fortune by selling sich wonderful wisdom!' said I. 'Oh, that's thrue,' he answered, 'but I always throw it around free to' dunces!'

As we neared the gap, I heard the well-known notes of a male lark. He was about fifty feet high. I stood in the lane. The lark was rising higher and higher. He was pouring out melody as if his heart would burst.

'That's him!' Michael said, as he stood admiring what he considered his private property.

Michael had a large face, he was square-jawed with a low brow, large nose, and a mouth that looked like an open oyster.

Ordinarily, that face looked about as spiritual as a rasher of bacon, but that morning in the lane it looked positively beautiful. There was a rapture on it as he looked at the lark, that shamed me into silence and put him in supreme command of the situation. Higher and higher rose the songster, and with him went Michael's stock! Fainter and fainter became the song, smaller and smaller became the rival of the nightingale, until he was a mere speck in the azure blue. Michael became poetic. He talked as if he were murmuring in a dream. As I watched and listened, conflicting emotions surged through me. I was under a spell. I was enraptured to the point of prayer or tears, and I was conscience-stricken that I had ever suspected Michael of 'a corner' in larks! I determined to atone for my sin. With upturned face I groped for his hand, and with it in mine we walked through a gap into the meadow.

'We'll see th' oul' hen if ye kape yer eyes open,' he said.

We seated ourselves closely together on a primrose bank. We sat there for about ten minutes.

75

The 'Oul' Man', as Michael called him, was still coruscating among the clouds—the river was at the other end of the meadow. We saw a kingfisher skim its surface, like a ball of fire; a wren twittered in a sloe bush near by; the air was laden with a perfume of flowers, and we basked in the sunshine—'Knee deep in June'.

The mother bird arrived. We watched her, with bated breath. She fluttered over our heads—she balanced herself about twenty feet from the ground, then darted over the river, balancing herself over an imaginary destination. Four times she performed the same illusory act in order to deceive us. Finally she alighted. Michael, of course, knew the spot, but was merely adding a little romance and poetry to the commercialism of the bargain. We went to the spot and found her front entrance—a flattened surface of a few inches wide, and from it a little arched Addison's Walk that led to the nest, containing four-flushed youngsters. We interrupted one of her many morning meals and the lady of the house screamed with indignation and excitedly cut capers over our heads. As if he had been shot out of a catapult, down came the father and joined in the rumpus. We hurried away from the scene—content.

That night, as I flew barefooted from house to house, with the evening papers, my footfall was light, my speech subdued, and I moved as if in a dream. Wherever I went, whatever I did, I could hear that song! As my body flitted in and out of the streets and alleys, my mind was in Gowdy's meadow!

I had earned the money from the larks. My father gave his consent, but as I climbed the ladder to my little pallet in the loft, he said: 'Keep yer eye on

Michael!' I brushed aside the suggestion as an evil thought. If I could have canonised Michael that night, I would have put him in the saints' calendar instanter! In the darkness I lay and cogitated on the sex probabilities of the larks. Two cocks and two hens was the average, of course, but suppose there were three cocks? One was all we could support. To whom should I present the other two? Then, of a nest of four, two usually died. Of course, in this case the hens being the weaker sex would die. All these things I pondered over in my sleepless mind. At no time in my musing, however, was the picture so dark or my luck so low as to dim my vision of a singing lark in Pogue's Entry. I pictured him cavorting around the little circular green spot in the cage and singing as his father sung that memorable morning. There had been no songster in our entry since the death of my father's old thrush—now we were on the eve of a renaissance, and my name was to the associated with the new order of things.

When the town clock struck the hour of midnight, I had everything arranged. I knew how everything would turn out—down to the most minute detail—I was happy—supremely happy!

I was awakened next morning at dawn by the cries of the fishermen as they drove through Antrim with their cart-loads of herring. Then I heard Barney Hugh's bread carts come lumbering down the street on their way to Ballymena.

In about three moves I was dressed and out. It was a beautiful morning. Con Mulholland, the night watchman, was just coming home with his gun on his shoulder. Old Billy O'Hare, the chimney sweep, went past on a dog-trot, like a little locomotive: puffs of tobacco smoke lingering in the track for a moment before dissolving in the still morning air.

Michael was a jack of all trades and master of one — manure monger — in a home-made cart he made a daily round of the streets, picking up manure for which he got a shilling a load. He called that his 'aisy money'.

I arose with the intention of helping him that morning, just to show my appreciation of his magnanimity. From the entrance to Pogue's Entry I could see south past the church, to Barney McQuillan's. To the north I could see past the town well, to Isaac George's at the townend. Michael was not within range of my vision. The condition of the street told me plainly that he had not worked at this vocation that morning. I went to his house. No one seemed to be up. I whistled. There was no response. I went around to the back of the house — I saw the dung cart — that reassured me.

After waiting about five minutes, I grew a little impatient and whistled 'The Boyne Water' with an assurance based on experience that if any of Michael's family were awake they would answer with a brickbat! Across the street a window was raised and Andy Lorimer poked his head out.

'Is that whistle for sale?' he asked in a wheezy voice — I moved away ashamed — Andy was in the last stages of consumption. In the absence of Michael I needed a bivalve to let off some of my pent-up emotion. I seized a couple of buckets and went to the town well for the family supply of water. Then I took the old heather besom and swept the mud floor. I was just putting the finishing touches to this work of supererogation when I heard a low whistle. I dropped the besom and joined Michael.

'Egad, I'm in throuble!' he said.

'What's the mather?' I asked.

'M' oul' maan wants me t' go scollopin' with 'im, an' if I can give 'im fourpence I can go fur th' larks instead.'

I fished out the price of the larks and handed it over.

'I'll meet you in Gowdy's meadow at two,' I said.

'No,' he replied, 'not in the meadow, meet me at the race, an' we'll haave a swim first—bring a good shivering bite.'

I announced in a rather important and self-conscious manner to my father that the larks were bought and paid for. I promised to have them home at three. He laughed.

'What 'er laughin' at?' I asked.

'Oh, nawthin',' he said, as he winked at my mother. I pulled out of the junk heap an old bird-cage—former home of the deceased cock thrush. I wiped it over with a dish-cloth and took it to Jamie Esler's. Jamie was finishing a coffin, but promised to add the lark's run in a day or two. The vison grew brighter and brighter every hour. Here was glory for Pogue's Entry, and the total cost was just sevenpence. After transacting business with the carpenter I went down town to Sam Johnson's bakery—Miss Elizabeth was at the counter—I had 'an account' there, and secured the shivering bite—half a bap and treacle. I stuffed the precious morsel into an inside pocket, and sighed for two o'clock! Time dragged on. At one o'clock I was on my way to the meadow. For the first time in my life, I deliberately threw away several chances to shoot marbles. I had a handful in my pocket, but I couldn't think of anything but larks. Pretty soon I arrived in the land of promise in *ne plus ultra* state of mind.

Perhaps *Gloria in Excelsis* would better express the mood. The appointment was to take place at the old swimming hole in the race, but as I passed the meadow, I thought there would be no betrayal of confidence in having a peep. Why shouldn't I? They were mine. As I reached the gap I saw a neighbour of mine—Johnny Adair, meandering around inside.

'Morrow, Johnny,' says I.

'Morrow, bhoy,' he answered, with a downcast, cadaverous look on his thin face.

'Going for a swim?' I ventured.

'After a while,' he replied, without looking at me. I determined to look at the larks anyway. I remembered the orientation: a straight line between the gap and a bare patch of sand on the opposite bank of the river—a tall ragweed bisected the line, and stood at the entrance to the nest.

'I'm going to take a danther over to the river,' I said, as I balanced myself for a straight dive for the nest.

'I'll stay,' said Johnny. I looked back. He was watching me. I went on. I scented danger in the presence of Johnny.

'Perhaps,' thought I, 'it would be just as well to take them with me.' I changed my mind—changed it several times before I reached the nest. I wasn't a foot out of my direction. The larks were gone—nest and all. For a moment I stood rooted to the spot—transfixed. A moment later my mind was at ease—Michael had taken them over to the old swimming hole! He would be there when I arrived. I was sure of that—as sure as mortal ever is of anything. I went on to the river. Behind a clump of blackberry vines sat Bob Doherty, bare-footed, splashing his feet in the river.

'Morrow, Bob,' I said cheerfully.

'Morrow,' he growled.

'Comin' over t' haave a dip?' I asked.

'Divil a dip,' was the curt reply. Bob asked a half a dozen questions in a breath—the last of which was the inquiry as to the whereabouts of Michael.

'No,' I said, 'I haaven't seen him, but I'm t' meet him at the race.'

'I'll bate ye a halfpenny he won't be there!' he said.

'I haaven't a halfpenny, Bob, but I'll bate ye half a bap an' treacle, he will!' Bob spat on his halfpenny, and slapped it into my open palm, as the manner of men is when they bind a bargain. I gave him a look at my collateral, and sat down beside him. We sat splashing in the water for a few minutes in silence. Bob stooped and picked from the bed of the river a section of the glacial period.

'See that stone?' he asked.

'Ay!'

'D'ye know what I'd like to with it?'

'No.'

'Jap th' brains out of that scallion-faced, flat-nosed grave robber!'

'Michael?'

'Ay, Michael.'

'Sure ye'd be hung,' says I.

'It 'ud be a luxury!' he answered, and followed the statement with a string of hair-raising and blasphemous expletives. Then he reported a catalogue of crimes committed, not only by Michael, but by his father, his grandfather, and his brother Bill.

A suspicion arose in my mind. I proposed that we go to the swimming hole. He agreed. As we went towards the race we noticed another well-known figure circumnavigating the ragweed. Bob's hate gave way to laughter. It was my turn to look careworn and anxious. Heedless of Bob's explosion, I joined Henry Kelly near the ragweed. Bob followed closely behind.

'Ye're lukin' fur something?' I asked.

'Ay,' Harry said. 'I'm lukin' fur a gully knife I lost th' other day.'

'Was it flushed?' Bob asked sarcastically.

'What 'er ye blethering about?' Harry asked innocently. Bob and I smiled at each other, and all three of us moved toward the race. When we reached the gap, Adair was still there.

'Here's the hardest worked man in th' town,' Bob said, 'studyin' nature.'

'Ay,' Johnny said. 'Human nayture.'

Suspicion increased in me, but my faith was equal to the strain. Michael's quondam friends were looking at the world through a nest of larks, and it looked back. They were dour and uncommunicative. We moved out of the gap and turned to the right toward the race. As we did, Tommy Wilson came along. We waited for him.

'Hallo, Tommy!' I hailed. 'Going for a plunge?'

'Ay,' he said; 'but I'm going into the meadow for a minute.'

'Did you lose a gully knife?' Bob asked.

'No; but I lost an oul' purse here th' other day.'

We stood in the lane and watched Tommy as he rounded the big ragweed in search of the nest. He took his cap off and scratched his head—we laughed outright. He heard us, and came slowly toward the lane with his hands in his pockets. Later, when he overtook us, he manifested a belligerent spirit. He suspected a conspiracy. We were all more or less of

the same mind, but no one openly expressed it. We laughed, and exchanged innuendoes, but every one ridiculed the idea that he was looking for larks.

Two minutes after we arrived at the swimming hole four of us were floundering around in the hole. Bob sat on the bank awaiting the result of the wager. Michael failed to appear. My half bap and treacle went the way of my hard-earned four pence. Bob did not condescend to hold the bap to my mouth while I took a mouthful. The others soon got into the secret and each took a bite. We compared notes and pooled our envy, hatred, malice, and all uncharitableness. We had been buncoed. There was no doubt of that. We invoked the aid of all the angels in heaven and all the devils in the other place to help us to get even with Michael. The price of the larks, we discovered, ranged from fourpence to a shilling. All had paid in advance, and faith was the essence of each contract. Schemes of revenge ranged from excommunication to tar and feathers. Each of us, one after another, offered to fight Michael, but neither as a remedy nor as revenge did that method appeal to us. He had a hide like a buffalo, and for a sixpenny consideration would volunteer to be thrashed every day in the week.

III

Fate threw us together a few days later. He had discreetly kept out of our way, but when Ned McCabe butchered John Coulon's pig Michael was on hand to enjoy the entertainment. A 'killing' was always an event in our community. On the anniversary of the Battle of the Boyne, the Protestants had their innings. On St Patrick's Day, the Romans had their's. Each creedal clan occupied the field to the exclusion of all others, but at a 'killing' we mixed as naturally as stirabout and buttermilk, and occupied reserved seats, together, irrespective of race, creed, colour, or previous condition of servitude.

There was an unusual crowd and good seats were at a premium. Ned was in the pig's sanctum sanctorum putting the snapper on the pig's snout, and as the first scream rent the air everybody scrambled for a seat, or standing room to view the performance. In looking hurriedly around, I saw Michael perched on the stone wall that overlooked the piggery. He beckoned me to a seat beside him on the wall. I looked around for men of Gowdy's meadow—not one of them seemed to be present. I climbed to Michael's side and greeted him in words not lawful to utter. Out came the pig, squealing, at the end of a rope. The crowd squeezed in around the sty. It was the crucial moment. Ned handed the rope to an assistant, took the big hatchet, swung it in the air with his powerful arms—thud! The rest was a kettle of boiling water and a scraper. A few lingered to see the details, but the majority dispersed.

As Michael and I got down from our seats on the wall, a husky young fellow by the name of McCague accosted Michael. 'Well,' says he, 'ye dilapidated hearse-driver, where's them larks?' Just then Johnny Adair hove in sight. 'Go on, Mac,' said he, even the score for the rest ov us!'

Off went McCague's coat and up went his shirt sleeves. Michael stood as undisturbed as a Sioux indian. A crowd gathered. Epithets, expletives, and threats flew thick and fast. With a vicious clout to the jaw McCague spun Michael around like a top.

The lark merchant was aroused. He hit Mac somewhere in the region of the solar plexus and doubled him up like a jack-knife. It was Adair's turn. Off went his coat and in he sailed. With one blow he closed one of Michael's eyes and with another he made the red fluid squirt in all directions out of Michael's big nose.

'Get a kettle of boilin' wather an' scrape 'im!' some one shouted. 'All I want is m' sixpence worth!' said Adair, as he battered away at a terrific pace. Michael had neither time to waste nor breath to spare, but he managed to blurt out: 'All this—fur—a—lousy—nest—of——.' He never finished the sentence; Adair did. He connected with Michael's organs of speech at the particular moment and a gutteral sound akin to that which Ned McCabe produced when he gave the pig its quietus, was the result. As the crowd saw Michael's legs give way, a reaction set in. Even those of us more intimately interested hoped he would rally and render a good account of himself, but he didn't and couldn't. When hope died within him he dropped on his knees to escape punishment. At this juncture a fair-haired girl of seventeen appeared on the scene. I must not give her name, for she is now the mother of a large family and a social leader in the community. 'Here,' she said, as she handed Michael the nest of larks, 'take them and give them back where they belong!' Michael could not see whether they were larks or cuckoos, but he held out his hands and took them. That instantly changed the base of activity.

'Here now,' said Michael, 'ye pack of dirty bloodhounds, take thim an' cut thim into bits an' divide them!'

Adair took them. He had worked the hardest for

86

them, but the rest of us closed in on him and each of us proposed a method of adjustment. One proposed to auction them, another to raffle them, and a third suggested that we draw lots. While we haggled over the adjustment the girl handed Michael her apron and he wiped the blood from his face and awaited developments. For the moment we forgot all about Michael. We finally resolved that as there was no hope of any refund, rebate, or return of the money, we would draw lots. Six of us had paid money, so we got six straws. We decided that the man who drew the shortest straw should get the larks. Three purchasers were absent. It was decided to draw for them.

'Come on,' she said, 'give the poor divil a chance! Haven't ye bate him yer money's worth—give him a straw, too!'

We looked at each other, then at the mutilated culprit, then at the girl. 'All right!' said the recuperated McCague. 'It's only once chance in seven; give it t' th' brute,' and a seventh straw was added.

The girl in the case held the straws. McCague drew first, then Adair tried his luck. I drew for the absentees.

'This,' said the girl, as she held up the last straw, 'is Michael's.'

'I'll be hung, dhrawn, an' quartered!' said McCague; 'if Michael hasn't got the larks.'

'It's the judgement of God,' Michael said, as he crossed himself. We considered it the judgement of a different kind of deity, but we moved away in disgust and chagrin!

It was mooted that there were others who should have participated in the drawing, but I had it from

Michael, on the quiet, that there was only one another, 'an' he,' said the lark man, 'is too much of a gintleman to make a rumpus over nawthin'.' I threatened to find him, and Michael gave me one of the larks to keep me quiet. He thought it was a hen, but it turned out to be a cock, and for some years enlivened Pogue's Entry with song.

Nearly thirty years later I was having a cup of tea with Sonny Johnston in Philadelphia. We were talking over old times in Antrim. 'The last time I saw you,' Sonny said, 'was in Gowdy's meadow.'

'What was I doing?' I asked.

'I don't know,' he replied; 'but I sat on one of the top branches of a chestnut-tree waiting for—— '

'Wating for Michael!' I interrupted.

'Ay,' he said; 'I paid him fur a nest av larks the day before, but he forgot to remember to bring them!'

Chapter 6

THE MIRACLE

I

It was a time of slackness. There were more workers than work, more cobblers than broken boots. Demand did not create supply. Poor folk like us are adept in the art of getting along on little, but living on nothing is something only fairies can accomplish, and we made sorry imitators. At the bottom we had no credit system—no reserve for rainy days. All days were wet in that respect, and 'sufficient unto the day is the evil thereof' was one of the doctrines we practised without faith.

Shoemakers cannot go out into the streets and examine the people's footwear. At least Jamie didn't. We blamed nobody. Nobody was to blame. There was nothing in the scheme of things as we knew it, that could provide work when there was no work to do. The ways of Providence to us were inscrutable. The State was still further removed from our ken. If we were conscious of any obligation to such an abstract thing, it was to keep out of jail. It never occurred to any of us that such an obligation might be mutual.

Hunger was never wholly a matter of misery. No casual visitor would ever have suspected we were starving. We never lost our sense of humour. I could have fought with a hungry dog for a bone, if there was anything on it, without shame, but to ask any one for a mouthful of bread would have been an eternal disgrace. To 'let on' was saying good-bye to what is called self-respect.

II

It was Wednesday morning. I was up early because a gnawing at the pit of my stomach would not permit me to sleep.

'Is there any hope th' day?' I asked Anna, as I was about to start for work.

'Oh, ay, dear,' she said cheerfully, 'there's always the chance of a miracle.'

It was the third day of the aching void. For a boy of my age I worked hard. The more energy I spent the keener I felt the need for supply. During the forenoon I worked as hard as ever. At noontime, while others were eating, I ran off to the woods to hide the fact that I had nothing to eat. I spent the noon hour thinking of ways and means. Part of my work was to feed cattle. I made up my mind to steal some of the turnips. The idea of eating while those at home had nothing, did not appeal to me. It looked mean. I changed my plans. I determined to give my scruples a rest and do something for the family.

I had been wondering what Anna meant by a miracle. In a hazy sort of way I imagined that it meant the supply of food by the help of God, but just how God could do it was a mystery. I got very weak in the afternoon. Out of such weakness comes desperation. I made up my mind to perform the miracle myself!

The hour and the place and the surroundings are as vividly fixed in my mind at this minute as they were then. My whole nature changed. If there is such a thing as a criminal mind, I became possessed of it at that minute. I looked upon all around me with suspicion. That is how they regarded me. I was sure of that. Something sprang into existence within me, something new and strange. I felt like a fox in the midst of a pack of hounds. Hunger had battered out of my mind all ethics, all morals, all religion. The right of property, always held up as sacred before me, vanished. Fear of jails, peelers, masters, laws, customs, and conventions had disappeared. With an agility and cunning born of despair, I planned the exploit. The darkness helped me. I secured the sack and crept stealthily out to the potato pit which was in a field, close to the land steward's house. I had helped to arrange this long pit. There were ten tons in it, and there were other pits of a similar size. When my conscience stung me, I quieted it by argument, by many arguments, each of them good, but not quite good enough. Here were potatoes for everybody, and plenty to spare. If I had asked I could certainly have had some as a gift, well, why not save my pride and take them?

I got down on my knees, and with my bare hands clawed away the earth. I took about a stone of them, covered the hole, and ran. Fifty yards away was the railway. Nobody walked there by night. It was too dangerous. That suited me. It was only a mile to the town, and I took my time. The perspiration poured down my face. I got nervous, and sat down on the potatoes for a rest.

When I reached the town head I put the sack under my arm and tried to look unconcerned. I quickened my steps and looked neither to the right nor to left. Of course, by this time the stone seemed a ton, but visions of the joy ahead gave me added strength.

Before entering, I cautiously looked through the window. The family were alone around the fire. In I walked and dropped the sack on the floor. A few faggots were burning on the heart, a candle burned in the sconce in her corner. They all looked and gasped.

'What's that?' Anna asked.

'It's th' miracle!' I said.

In that instant I realised what I was up against, but I depended on their hunger helping me out. Jamie muttered something. I didn't hear it. I was waiting for *her* judgment. That was final. If she gave in I was all right, and we would feast and be merry. If she stood firm I was lost. My sister arose to get them. Anna pressed her back on her stool. Jamie looked at me, then looked at my mother. The moment was intense. Hunger was acute. Nature was in revolt.

'Son o' mine,' she said in a trembling tone, '*you* wouldn't break yer oul' mother's heart, wud ye?' The words cut me like a knife. The soft emphasis on '*you*' aroused in me bitter resentment.

'We're starvin' t' death!' I yelled, as I stamped my bare foot on the mud floor. 'They've got plenty out there! Everybody's got plenty, an' I tuk them, an' we'll keep them, an' ate them.' And I dropped on the floor beside the sack and burst into tears. There was a moment's silence. Then I began again to protest.

'Silence, you!' Jamie shouted in a voice that made me shiver from head to foot. I heard her sigh. Ah, that deep sigh, which was the forerunner of a sob! I think I hear it now.

She took her apron in her hands and covered her

face. Our hearts sunk within us. Jamie made a move towards me, in anger, but she put a hand out and held him on his seat.

'Get me my little shawl, Mary.'

I knew what was in her mind, and as quick as a flash I arose, seized the sack, and fled into the darkness.

III

The front street had few lamps, but they were burning more brightly than usual. I kept out of their glare as much as possible. I avoided people as I avoided light. I feared to meet the boys who knew me more than I feared the police. My face was tear-streaked, and I would have to explain it or fight. I invented a dozen excuses or explanations, none of which either excused or explained. I was full of remorse, and the potatoes were now as heavy and cumbersome as a dead elephant.

From one side of the street to the other I went, courting the shadows. Sometimes the sack was over my shoulder, at other times under my arm.

When I reached the railway bridge at the edge of the town, I put the potatoes on the bridge wall and climbed up beside them to plan out this remorseful purgatorial journey. I recalled the number of men killed on the railway, and not knowing anything about the train schedule, I decided to take the road. Con Mulholland, the night watchman, carried a gun. I had seen him load it, and I feared Con more than I feared the police.

Again I shouldered the sack and started. The road was rough, the night was dark as pitch. I kept as near the middle of the road as I could. The sharp stones made walking painful. I tried the footpath. It

93

was soft to my bare feet, but I forgot the little gullies and went headlong over one. Farren's farm-house was half-way to my destination; when I got within a hundred yards of it the dog barked. I felt for a stone, just as a matter of precaution. The beast kept barking until I got hundreds of yards beyond.

There was a little hill on the right that I used to know as the 'Fairy Mountain'. I knew the fairies lived there. What would they think of me? Perhaps they, too, stole when they were hungry! Oh, no, that was impossible, for they could perform real miracles. Besides, if they were hard up they had the leprauchan.

As I drew near, I imagined myself before one of their judges. I invented my defence, but it wasn't convincing. No, the fairies could not be fooled. I heard sounds. The cold sweat broke out on my brow, and the potatoes now felt as heavy as cobble stones. My legs grew weaker, but if I dropped there it would be like an invitation to them to come and carry me off. I pressed on, quickening my pace into a dog-trot.

Half a mile ahead there was a bend in the road. Just as I felt assured that the fairies had ignored me, a carriage with two glaring lamps turned the bend of the road and came tearing towards me. I knew all the coachmen within ten miles. They knew me. The lamps lit up every inch of the road as they passed. I threw the potatoes on my back and pulling the loose end of the sack over my head, walked as close to the hedge as I could get.

When the carriage passed, I sat down on the roadside. The perspiration had made sodden wet every rag of clothing on my body. I stretched myself at full length on my back, and lay with my head on

94

the potatoes. Here a new mental disturbance diverted me from my remorse and agony for a while. Just about where I lay, I met every morning for months a little girl who made an early journey to Antrim daily in order to catch the early train for Belfast. She was studying music. One day I nerved myself up to the point of asking Withero who she was. The stone-breaker's reply was so brutal that I almost resolved never to carry his hammers home again.

'Yis, of coorse,' said he, 'she's the chile of Misther Seeds, an' ye'd bether save yer sheep's eyes fur somethin' more common. They're quality, ye know!'

Despite this wet-blanket advice of the cynic, I looked forward with increasing interest to this daily inspiration.

If she could see me now, what would she think? Of course, I had never spoken to her, my hopes never rose to that height, but what did that matter? The look in my mother's eyes filled me with remorse, but if the little girl in the pink dress could see me I would feel unfit to live.

I resolved there and then that if I got out of this awful scrape I would save up somehow and get a pair of boots and a hard hat—the hat first, so that if she ever spoke to me I could raise it politely.

The rest cooled my clothes. They now hung round me like cold, wet dish rags, and I shivered. I pulled myself together and pushed on. I was in the danger zone. Bleaching greens were all round me, and Con was standing in some corner with his gun all ready. He was reputed to have the eyes of a cat and the scent of a setter dog.

My fear increased as I neared the bend of the road. I put the sack down and put my ear to the ground. I knew Indians did that. I heard sounds. They were indistinct, but disquieting enought to further shake my nerves. I was weak, my steps were slow, and my hair felt as if it was standing straight up. For the first time I wavered in my intention to put the potatoes back. I thought of throwing them over the hedge and completing the job in the morning. That would involve a lie, and my mother could look right into the centre of my soul and see its blackness.

We had two books at home. One was an old backless bible, and the other a copy of *Pilgrim's Progress*. I called to mind the woodcut where Pilgrim stands at the gate with his pack upon his back. I remembered that Anna had spelled out to me the words over the gate. 'Knock, and it shall be opened unto you.' I wondered what Pilgrim had in his pack. Anna said he had sins in it. I wondered if God charged me with a sin for each potato or whether the whole business counted as one big potato sin? I began to count my sins. Jamie said whistling on Sunday was a sin. If that was so, what was the use of counting? I had enough sins of that character to burn me to ashes without the potatoes.

I turned the bend in the road. The old Quaker graveyard was right there. I dreaded to pass it. That was where Hughie Thronton had seen a banshee. If she turned up, I was sure she would scare me to death, and if I was found dead beside the sack next morning, all the world would know of my sin. As I passed the gate I tried to persuade myself that ghosts and fairies and banshees were all humbug. My feigned scepticism didn't work. My head pained me, my legs grew weaker, and I felt as if I was about to faint. I had only fifty yards to go now, but they seemed fifty miles.

I held my breath and listened before making a final dash for the potato pit. Not a sound could be heard save the rustling of the leaves of the trees. As I crept stealthily along, I stepped on a sharp stone and fell. For a minute or two I was unable to rise. It was too late to go back. The pain in my head grew intense, but I arose and staggered the rest of the way. I had to push a gate open to enter the field. It creaked. I was sure the noise could be heard a mile away. I waited a minute and then went through, and in a few seconds was sitting beside the hole in the pit. Just as I had put them back and scraped the earth over the hole, I heard voices. The road was only a few yards away, but a wall stood between. The voices grew more and more distinct.

Some man had escorted home to the land steward's house a young lady who was staying there. The little garden gate was within ten yards of the potato pit. They stopped at the gate. I held my breath again. They could hear me breathe if they listened, and they were too busy. They kept laughing and kissing. I thought they would never part. What idiots! I thought. I couldn't move. I dare hardly breathe, and they kept on and on! Then nature gave out, exhaustion flattened me out on my back, and I fell asleep.

IV

When I awoke everything was as still as the grave. The darkness was more intense than ever. Horrible dreams had haunted me. Ghosts had come trooping out of the Quaker graveyard. I had been chased and captured several times, but somehow I always escaped. In this chaotic nightmare Con Mulholland figured prominently with his gun. The dog at

Farren's farm was there too. I knew nothing of the time. I could not tell how long I had slept. Every joint in my body seemed like the rusty hinges of the gate that creaked.

When I reached the road I felt as free as a bird. The fearful crime was as though it had never been committed. I was on the king's highway, and the potatoes were in the pit, and who could swear that they had ever been out? I invented a whole catalogue of lies to tell any peeler, watchman, or banshee if they held me up! I had a right on the king's highway, it was the only right I had, or thought I had. Of course, being on it at midnight might make a difference. If so, that's where the lies would come in handy.

On the return journey I was engrossed with conflicting emotions. The burden was gone, and I felt as if I was walking on air. When I passed the Quaker graveyard and the 'Fairy Mountain' and Farren's farm, I imagined all sorts of grusome happenings. Past each of these places I ran as fast as my weak legs would permit me. I couldn't run very fast. It was so dark, and I was weak, but the sprihting was quite a creditable performance.

The town lamps were out. I groped my way with my bare feet down the street. Not a sound could be heard, not a light was visible. As I neared Pogue's Entry, I groped along the walls of the houses. Within a few doors of my home I began to feel like a drunken person. I was dazed, and began to reel and stagger. As I laid my hands on the entrance of the entry, I touched a human form!

The touch unnerved me, and I utterly collapsed. The human was my mother, who was keeping her vigil for the return of the prodigal.

Next morning my mother came up the little ladder to the half loft and aroused me. The gnawing pain of hunger was keen, but her face was smiling again.

'It was jist nothin' but a bad dhrame, dear,' she said, as she kissed me and sent me off to work.

Ah! what a beautiful world I entered that morning! How beautifully the birds sang, and how kind the trees were!

Chapter 7

A CANDLE IN THE WINDOW

I

I never knew what started the trouble. But that a great sorrow had come I could tell by the dazed look on her face. Something had happened to an elder brother of mine. He did not come to supper, and his stool at Anna's request was left vacant.

Folk who think little, adjust themselves easily to any change of circumstance, and as Anna did most of the thinking for our family she adopted the method of the vacant stool to acquaint us with the fact that something had gone wrong.

It was inevitable, of course, that my elder brother should go out into the larger world sometime, but to leave in a 'huff' was what hurt her heart. Besides, there was no room in such small quarters for grown-up men. It was something bordering on the miraculous how we got along as well as we did.

If he had left the town we would have been saved the shame of his taking lodgings with the Bennets.

My brother had a tender heart, and a tongue that was always tipped with kindness. No angry word had ever passed between him and my mother. My father, toward the grown-up sons, was generous to a fault. In fact, there came a time when the word of my elder brother was law in our household. Knowing all that, we were mystified when the rupture of relations came.

Not a word passed the lips of the old people in criticism. It was the biggest burden of sorrow I had ever seen there—a sorrow that bound them together in a new way. Jamie's tones became more tender. We could not escape it, for when Anna had sorrow we saw it on her face, and a pall hung over the temperament of the household.

When she learned that he had taken up lodgings at the Bennets, she sent a note to him. It was written at the back window beside the bed. She had written letters to a sister of mine who was first to leave the home; but this was the first she had written to a son. Years afterwards he told me about it. The only thing in it that he remembered was her promise to have a candle in the window every night until he returned.

We were all rough-hewn people, and the fine edges were few and hard to find. My brother was a labourer, and his life and language was devoid of an idealism that overtook him later in life. He didn't give the incident much thought, because, perhaps, he was unaware of the nature of the soul from whom he had abruptly severed himself. That was a failing common to all.

I was an eye-witness of the installation of the first candle. It was a sensational episode. It was a common halfpenny 'dip'. She lit it, and sticking it to the bottom of a small plate, placed it in the front window. Then she returned to her chimney corner and sat alone beside the smouldering embers until it had burnt itself out.

There were four houses in our entry. Directly opposite lived McGrath, the rag man. Next door to him lived O'Hare, the chimney-sweep. Mary McConaghy lived next door to us.

The candle, though small, lit up the whole front of

McGrath's house. They went to bed at dusk every night. None of us had ever seen a light in their house. McGrath's wife and daughter shared the ragman's philosophy that darkness was intended for sleep and daylight for work, so they went to bed in the twilight, and arose with the first gray light of dawn. So they were not disturbed by the candle. That could not be said of us, however. The light could not penetrate the bedroom when the door was shut, but, weak and yellow though the rays were, they lit up the rest of our house, and it was some time before we could get accustomed to it. I lay in the loft, under the roof beams, and the rays of the candle, combined with the mystery of the arrangement, made it at first difficult to go to sleep.

I did not need to be told the meaning of the candle. I knew it as plainly by instinct as if I had been informed of the details. I found myself listening for his footfalls coming down the entry, night after night. I could never see her face, but I heard deep sighs, and at times imagined I heard smothered sobs. Perhaps I was mistaken. She did talk—but not to him.

II

The nightly vigil was one of those incidents that could not be long hidden from the notice of the neighbours. In a few days everybody around us knew about it. Those to whom any gossip was a sweet morsel came in to express sorrow. Anna never discussed the subject with any of them. She discussed it very little with Jamie. He tried by all the means in his power to persuade her to abandon it—or at least to retire and let the candle alone do the silent watching.

103

'I've never asked for things ye hadn't t' give, haave I, Jamie?'

'Oh, no, no, it's not that—it's fur yer own sake, Anna.'

'Then please let alone—th' heart sorrow is all I can bear, and—'

'I shall say no more, Anna, not a —— word!'

We all hoped that Sunday would bring a change. He would have the day off, and would surely call and relieve the tension. Anna arrayed herself in her best linen cap, and the house was given a special 'reddin' ' up.

We had callers all the afternoon. Every footfall on the cobble stones startled us for a moment. We knew who was coming by the sound of their brogues. His footfall was one of the most familiar.

He didn't come. None of us made any remarks about his failure. As the shadows of evening began to fall Anna put the kettle on and prepared the supper. We had no visitors then, and feeling that she would be more pained than usual, we were glad to be alone.

To our astonishment she seemed in lighter vein than she had been in for months. Her repartee was more subtle and humorous. Her laugh was contagious. We were not always aware of the fine points, but we laughed because she laughed. Jamie's face was a study. It glowed.

'Yer heart's not so sore,' he ventured to say quietly.

'It gets sorer every day, dear, but I'm learnin' m' lesson.'

'Ay, well, we're niver too ould t' learn, Anna, are we?'

'No. But it came t' me all of a sudden that I was

104

jist doin' t' you and th' wains what m' poor boy unbeknownst t' himself was doin' t' me.'

'Acushla, we're more consarned about you than about him—ye see he's young, an he's got them fellahs about him.'

'M' cloud of sorrow will no longer darken your heart, Jamie. A love that seeks jist what belongs to itself is pure selfishness, with a nicely named cloak thrown around its shoulders!'

'Ay,' Jamie said, 'we niver know what's under a high hat or shufflin' along in a pair ov brogues!'

'There's jist Wan that Knows.'

'Ah, ay, ov coorse, but He's God, an' He dizn't let on!'

The glory of the Celtic mind whether in literature or in life is in its moods. Ephemeral it may be, and fluid.

Anna's face reflected all her moods. Her look would smite us with an unspeakable sorrow and a minute later we would observe a change that would provoke laughter. In this case she played a part. Her poignant heart agony was hidden behind a smiling face. The lighter mood made no change in the arrangements. That night, when the curfew bell had tolled and we had retired, the candle was placed in the window as usual. Jamie remained in the corner until the wick collapsed in the tallow and the vigil was over for the night.

It was inevitable that my brother should hear about the welcome light that spoke so eloquently of a heart that was dark with sorrow. The news did not soften him. It was not that he was hard. He had, perhaps, grown weary of home restraint, and now that he had broken away he was not pleased to be told that his absence had furnished the whole neighbourhood with gossip.

He intended to come, but he put it off again and again. He resented being told that he had a duty there. He intended to send word or write a note in the meantime; but that also he postponed to a more convenient season. It was our first family problem of a filial nature. So little would have healed the breach. The longer it was postponed the harder it became. The poor are disciplined by necessity. They pay heavy penalties for ignorance. Our lives at certain stages are guided by impulse. There is a lack of finesse. The amenities are crude because we have only a cash nexus with those to whom social intercourse is part of the fine art of living.

At the very core of our natures we possess the essentials—the materials—for things high and fine and noble. We demonstrate all that when we get a chance, but that rarely occurs.

A fine-strung nature amongst us, therefore, is often roughly handled, not because we are more brutal than any other class, but because the rough edges of our primordial instincts have little chance of being smoothed by the refining influence of whatever culture there may be around us.

III

We soon became accustomed to what Jamie called 'her notion'. We never imagined that her frail body would get tired. One morning as I sat up on my straw pallet and looked over the edge of the loft into the chimney corner, I saw a sight that produced my first great fear. Anna was lying flat on her back on the mud floor. Her arms were extended, and she looked very white. I stopped breathing for a minute to listen. I could hear no sound. I swiftly descended the little ladder, and rushing into the bedroom, aroused Jamie. Fear had deprived me of speech, but when Jamie saw the terror in my face he needed no explanation. In a moment he was at her side.

'Ye divil's imp!' he said to me, as she opened her eyes, 'ye scared the sowl out o' me!'

'I jist fell asleep, dear,' she said.

'Ay, but shure thon fella'll be th' death o' ye, wuman,' he said, as he took her arm and helped her to her stool.

As she rose I noticed something in her hand. She saw me looking at it, and quickly thrust her hand beneath her apron.

An uncanny sort of feeling came over me. Had the fairies visited her in the night? I wondered. She brought her hand out, but it was empty. I knew whatever it was she had left it on her lap.

Jamie was inclined to be gruff at first, but the soft look in her eyes made him ashamed, and he worked his gruffness off on me.

'Here,' says he, 'don't stand there like a stuck pig lukin' at yer mother—get some sticks t' light th' fire!'

'Don't ate his head off, Jamie.'

'Ah cudn't, Anne,' he said, with a softening tone, 'it's wuden.'

I got sticks and peat and proceeded to light the fire, but I kept a sharp eye on her lap. Jamie filled the kettle, and hung it on the chain, and then coaxed her to go to bed.

'If ye'll jist lie down an' haave forty winks. Ah'll make ye a cup o' tay that'll make ye ten years younger—Ah will that.'

'Ye're a brave maan, Jamie, but jist make it nine, an' give me th' tay first.'

As I struck a match to light the fire Anna rose,

107

and, forgetting about what she had hidden from my curiosity, it dropped on the floor. She snatched it up instantly, but too late. The secret was out. It was a baby's shoe—*his* shoe, the first he had ever worn.

'It's quare,' said Jamie in a kindly tone, 'how we bamboozle ourselves when we're thinkin' long.'

'Ay, dear, it's th' ould question of a dhrownin' maan clutchin' at a straw—only in this case it's a sinkin' ould crayther of a wuman puttin' all her nice memories into a baby's boot.'

'He's a mane baste, an'll weep salt tears some o' these days,' said Jamie indignantly.

'We're all spun out o' th' same yarn, Jamie. He's jist doin' what we all do, an' do every day.'

'An' what might that be, if ye plaze?'

'Oh, jist forgettin' t' be nice.'

At last the vigil ended. The candle no longer lit up the wee shop of Pogue's Entry. It had burned there only for a few weeks anyway.

Then he came and kissed her good-bye before he left for Scotland.

To my brother, the incident at the time was a matter of no importance at all. Years later he saw it from her point of view. As he mingled with men and women he began to understand something of the tenderness of a mother's heart. In his letters he began to express a little of this new understanding. Not much, however, for, like my father, 'soft words' to him were weak and for feminine use. He made up his mind to tell her himself, some day, how bitterly he had regretted the candle incident, but just as he put off walking across the street and ending the vigil, so he postponed the fulfilment of his good intentions, until one day he walked into our little cottage in Pogue's Entry and saw her lying in her coffin.

Many years afterwards he told me of that last visit. It is many years since he followed her into the unknown, but his words are still ringing in my ears.

'It wasn't the fact that she was dead—we've all got to go that way,' he said in a vacant sort of way. 'It was something that cut deeper than that. It was a shadow over my heart. I seemed to stand between a lighted candle and her cold, white face, but the shadow fell on my heart.

'I couldn't get away from the candle. Night and day it was there. There was much to do, for father was as helpless as a baby. He wouldn't accept death. He talked to her just as usual. In the middle of the night—the night of the wake—the little crowd of neighbours who sat around the hearth had a cup of tea—Jamie took his cup into the room, and we heard him say, "Anna, dear, won't ye haave jist a wee sup?"

'I looked around toward the window and there stood the candle burning as brightly as it did when I was breaking her heart. Ah, God, the agony of that light burning in my mind! I did not speak of it. Nobody there would have understood. Looking into that dear white face for the last time was agony. Trying to soothe and quiet the old man was heartrending. To listen to the words of the neighbours, to hear the sobs and see their tears, tried my strength; but all of them combined was as nothing compared to the pain of that mental image of a burning candle in that little window!

'Years later I ceased to be pained by its appearance. I learned to look upon it as her welcome light on the pathway to that other home where there shall be no more crying and all tears shall have been wiped away.'

Chapter 8

THE COMING OF THE LAMP

I

The Wilsons had a lamp two years before we seriously considered giving up candles. A lamp seemed beyond our reach, anyway, and even apart from the question of finance, my father had worked by the light of tallow candles for over a generation. Jamie didn't want to be accused of slavishly imitating a neighbour.

When a customer suggested a lamp, he would avoid the discussion. If he couldn't avoid it he would use his stock arguments:

'They're too dangerous, an' they say if ye dhrop a match in th' oil, ye'd blow th' house up.'

'An' wouldn't that same happen if ye dhropped it in gun-powdther?'

'Ay, to be sure, but we're not usin' gun powdther.'

Continued suggestions had their effect upon him. He had always said he would burn candles while he lived. He had to confess to Anna, however, that the Wilson's lamp was a wonder, filling the room with a white light. Anna was for a lamp. He was obdurate. About once a week the thing was mentioned in a casual way. One day Mrs Wilson came in, and Anna drew from her the comparative prices of lamps and candles.

The lamp was cheaper. 'But,' Mrs Wilson said, 'if

it was ten times as dear we wouldn't go back to candles.'

I think this convincing colloquy was staged by Anna just as an extra vigorous suggestion for Jamie.

'If there was aany wan here who could work the d——d thing,' he said one day, 'I wouldn't mind, maybe.'

We'd jist haave to learn like the Wilsons, dear,' Anna replied.

'Ay, I know rightly they had, but there was a time when they hadn't it.'

'We've no place t' hang it.'

'Shure it's aisy enough to hammer a nail in the roof.'

'What's the use, whin I'm jist totterin' to th' grave, anyway?'

If it's as dark as they say it is, Jamie, the whiter the light the betther, and forby, shure Jamie Wilson is totterin' in th' same direction.'

'M' mind's all throughother wi' yer argyments, Anna, an' I've got this sole t' finish,' was his parting shot.

Jamie became thoroughly convinced that a lamp gave better light than a candle. He was convinced that it was cheaper. The trouble was in his obstinacy. He didn't want to give in. He knew he would have to do so, but he would hold out as long as he could.

The question of lamp or no lamp became a vital issue in our domestic affairs. We boys and girls kept extolling the glories of the Wilson lamp. We gave Jamie little peace. Being as convinced as we were, he became less and less irritated.

'Ye've all got lamps on the brain,' he said one night; 'ye'd think ye were all born in a lamp shop t'

111

hear ye! Ye'd luk fine if ye were all blown out ov th'
roof and come down in bits—wudn't ye now?'

We laughed loudly. Anna laughed too, and
remarked:

'You'd have to borrow a lamp to gather up the
fragments, Jamie!'

There came a time when the problem was no longer
one of the relative merits or comparative cost. When
Jamie said to Anna:

'Well, ye might find out th' cost ov this
new-fangled notion,' we knew the battle was won.

Down to William Vance's we went *en masse.*

'We're goin' to haave a lamp,' I said to Bill Gainer
as I went along.

'Why don't ye go in fur gas?' said Bill, with a turn
of his nose.

Going and coming I must have told at least a score
of boys.

Sensations like that had a way of spreading in our
quarter, where everybody knew or wanted to know
everybody else's business. When we returned we
were furnished with all the information the town
afforded on lamps, wicks, and oil. Years later Jamie
confessed that nothing of this was news to him, for
one day, unknown to us he had sneaked into Vance's
and inquired all about them himself.

The next step was the money to buy the lamp.
That was a real difficulty. The house began to
retrench and save. I was selling newspapers at the
time, and the prospect of a lamp increased my
energy. I found myself really caring whether people
bought papers or not.

It took nearly a month to arrive at 'The Day'.
When we arrived, Jamie himself went for it. He
warned us not to follow him. Any one of us found on

the street was to have the stirrup! Well, if we got the lamp, that wouldn't matter, but we kept clear of him. We followed at a distance. We watched him enter the shop.

It seemed as if it took him hours to buy that lamp. Two sisters and I stood at the church gate with our eyes riveted on Vance's door.

Finally he came with a box under his arm, and we moved back towards Pogue's Entry—casting furtive glances backward to watch his movements.

Jamie carried that lamp as if it was the ark of the covenant. Coming through High Street no one took any notice, but when he came as far as John Darragh's blacksmith's shop the neighbours were at the doors. Not all of them. I had not time to alarm the whole upper part of the town. He had a cutty pipe in his mouth, just to help him look unconcerned. When he was within a hundred yards we ran down the entry and alarmed Anna.

'Whisht, dear, keep quiet,' was all she said, but she was just as excited as any of us.

Before the box was opened the neighbours were discussing it at the mouth of the entry. Some of the more familiar ones ventured over the doorstep, just to offer a few remarks on the weather. Jamie was untying the strings when Anna arose, and taking the box, passed into the bedroom and, depositing it on the window, returned to entertain the visitors. Jamie lit his pipe and sat down on the bench and began to work. We were irritated, but a look at Anna's face was all the explanation we needed.

II

The social code of the bottom of the world is quite flexible, the amenities are rather crude. Our neighbours used our front door as if it had been the gate of a public park. But nature makes up for what human nature leaves undone.

We all had keen intuitions, and the intuitive faculty cleared our house in five minutes. They did not need to be told to go. They went.

When the house was cleared, Jamie shut the door and barred it. Then the box was produced and we gathered around.

'Be careful of the chimney!' said Anna, as Jamie drew it forth first.

'Oh, don't be afraid,' he said. 'I handled half a dozen while I was in the shop jist fur practice.'

'Did they show ye how to light it?'

'No!'

'Why?'

'D'ye think I'd make an exhibition ov m' ignorance t' Vance?'

Carefully the parts were laid out on the table. A piece of wick stuck in the burner. Jamie screwed it on the reservoir. Anna took the chimney and adjusted it, and Jamie struck a match to light it.

'Ye've forgot something, dear.'

'What?'

'Oil.'

Jamie scratched his head and smiled.

'Ay, ye're right for once,' he said, and then looking at her he continued in an abstract sort of way:

'Will ye iver forget the first box of matches we iver seen?'

'I mind it rightly.'

'Ha, ha!' he laughed, 'they got wet and we put them close to the fire to dhry, an' off they went! Ha, ha! Well, well, well——.'

'Oil, Jamie, oil, dear. We can't keep that door barred all day, ye know.'

Oil cans were discussed. Wilsons, of course, had one. The financial situation was canvassed. We didn't know the exact price of them, but we knew that the exchequer could not at that juncture bear the strain. Being most fleet of foot, I was despatched with a jug for our first pint of oil.

It was with difficulty that I squeezed through the neighbours who crowded the narrow entry. Everybody knew my mission. I told them! Two pals—favourites, were on the street. I took them along.

Down through the town we sped for the oil. I could have gotten it at Farren's, a few hundred yards away, but, as Jamie would say, we had Vance on the brain.

Jamie had over-estimated the price of oil. I had a penny too much. 'Bob,' one of the pals, suggested a stick of barley sugar. I hesitated. Vance might have under-charged, and would demand the penny later, and my pantaloons were thin. I stoutly resisted—not on moral scruples, but because I knew Jamie.

As we came up past the church a lad named Scott stepped in front of me, and wanted to settle an old score.

I couldn't settle. I hadn't a marble in my possession.

'Fight 'im!' said Bob. 'Go on! I'll hold the oil.'

I thought of the barred door and the waiting family. A scrap was a tame affair compared to the lamp, and I demurred. As I moved on, Scott held his arm up and spat over it. The Irishman never lived who could refuse that most aggravating of all challenges and live it down! I handed the oil to Bob and mixed it with Scott. A crowd gathered and

115

egged us on; we were both winded and spent when some one shouted:

'Skip! there's a peeler.'

'We'll be at Pigeon Hill th' morra afthernoon,' said Bob to Scott, as I wiped the blood from my nose and ran up town.

'What the —— —— kept ye?' said Jamie impatiently, as he opened the door.

'The shop was full o' people!' I said in a tone of injured innocence.

'Which ov them tore yer shirt, dear?' Anna asked, as she critically looked me over.

Happily for me, Jamie was too much engrossed with the lamp to notice the remark. He was filling the reservoir. That done, he wiped his hands behind the front of his trousers and screwed on the burner. Anna lit it, and he adjusted the chimney. Somebody knocked.

'Let them dundther! said Jamie, as the flame shot up through the glass.

Something went wrong. The thing smoked. We were all excited. The chimney must be removed. Instinctively we all saw that at the same moment.

Jamie took the chimney in his hand. He didn't hold it long.

'Phewt—Jazus!' he exclaimed. 'I've roasted m' hand off!' and the chimney dropped in fragments on the mud floor.

'Here endeth the first lesson,' said Anna, as she picked up the bits of glass and threw them behind the burning peat. Jamie turned down the flame. Nobody said anything, but we all saw clearly that if he had done it sooner he would have saved himself and the chimney.

'I knew it—I was sure ov it from the start,' he

117

said. 'I'm goin' back t' candles, an' stick t' them till I die.'

Our hearts sank within us, but Anna, always the champion of hope, always the discoverer of silver linings, revived our drooping spirits. Jamie abandoned the project. He sat down at his bench and went on with his work. Anna whispered something to Mary. I didn't hear what it was, but Jamie seemed to know, for he arose from the bench and raised his voice in protest. That raised voice always made us shiver—not because it meant anything in particular, but because it could be heard outside in the entry.

'No, no,' said he, 'ye will not ask Misthress Wilson, nor Misther Wilson, nor Misther Vance aither, t' come in here and examine our ignorance. If ye do, jist as sure as gun's iron, I'll take the whole d——d prakus an' dance on it! I will that!'

'As ye had a little practice in handlin' them, Jamie, maybe ye'd like a wee bit of practice in dancin' on these bits first.'

'It's no laughin' matter.'

'No, dear, nor dancin' matther aither.'

III

Jamie lit his pipe and smoked as he hammered. Anna gathered up the lamp and removed the activities to her bedroom. She opened the front door and let those who were burning up with curiosity venture in. She then went into her room and shut the door. We followed.

Instead of proceeding with lamp arrangements, she took the money out of her little leather purse and looked at it. She didn't count it. She knew how many pennies were there. They hadn't increased. She was just swithering what to do. We saw the problem on her face, and were already voting for the chimney.

Jamie was pretending to be in high dudgeon, but he knew in his heart that the problem would not end where he left it. In a few minutes he joined us in the bedroom and shut the door after him.

'Well,' he grunted, 'are ye still crackin' yer brains over bein' quality an' haavin' a lamp jist because th' Wilsons have one?'

'No, dear,' Anna said, 'we have decided that. We are jist tryin' to make up our minds whether we'll have light for supper—or porridge.'

'We'll have porridge!' said Jamie.

'I think we'll haave light, dear.'

'It's a mortal pity there isn't an extra pair ov trousers in th' house. Ye might put them on jist to show yer authority,' he replied tartly.

'Shure it's brains and good sense we need, Jamie, an' if throusers don't give them to you, they wouldn't be likely to give them to me, aither.'

'Egad, it's quare what odd notions wimin do haave these days,' he answered, as he went out and resumed his work at the bench.

'What haave ye in yer pockets?' Anna asked me.

'A peerie and sthring, an' four marbles an' a catapult,' I answered, with some curiosity and alarm.

'Lave them all on that window sill an' run to Vance's for a new chimney for the lamp.'

The news that we had failed got noised abroad in the entry somehow, and as I came out with my face aglow and eyes sparkling with excitement, the curious eyed me critically and followed my movements until I was out of sight.

While I was gone, Anna had performed a miracle. She had persuaded Jamie to hammer a stout nail in a rafter of the roof—just over his bench.

'It's not that I'm givin' in,' he said, 'but jist because I know that whin a woman makes her mind on somethin' her tongue keeps waggin' on't like a wheel without a cog—ay, that's jist it, now ye have it.'

But he took care that it was the right kind of nail, and that it was so driven that a lamp could not be safely suspended therefrom. I had left the house under the impression that supper money had gone into the lamp chimney, but Anna had resources that often baffled us. When I returned she was preparing supper. Of course it wasn't the regular ration, but it was supper.

In the twilight Jamie got his old candlestick as usual and arranged the big penny candle in it—a sort of notice to the family that he was determined to hold out to the last ditch.

The parts of the lamp, with the new chimney, were laid out on the bed, and we were ordered out of the bedroom, and the door was closed. Operations were suspended until the neighbours who still hung around got tired, and we had our evening meal.

Hardly a word was spoken that night at supper. We children were excited still—full of pent-up emotion. Towards the close of this abbreviated meal hour we were informed by Anna that outside curiosity was not to be satisfied that night.

'It's no use glunchin',' Jamie said, as he watched the disappointment spread over our faces.

'Is Mrs Wilson goin' t' show ye how t' light it?' Mary asked.

'She isn't!' Jamie said, as he glowered at her.

Here was another mystery. Jamie and Anna had evidently struck a compromise—and we had not been informed. We couldn't go out then? We had nothing to tell.

When the town clock struck nine, and Sammy Cooper tolled out the days of the month, we had to go to bed—always. That night, for the first time in my memory, the hours dragged along at an aggravatingly slow pace. Jamie worked at the bench, and Anna was evidently not feeling so badly, for he sung 'Black Eyed Susan' and The Old Gray Mare' that night. The world was always swinging round correctly on its axis when Jamie sung. Anna evidently was pleased. We could tell that by her face. There was nothing for us to do but grin and bear it—for a night.

As I lay on my pallet that night in the little half loft I became suspicious that the old folk were going to put that lamp up during the night and rob us of the sensation of being in at the start. They sat at the turf fire, talking in an undertone. From the sound of Jamie's voice I knew that the storm had passed. The forces of reform and reaction had triumphed—the lion and the lamb were comparing notes!

With but a slight movement of my head I could look over the edge of the loft and see them at the fire. There was a candle in the little tin sconce in her corner, and Jamie had put on a few extra clods of peat. The *Weekly Budget* had been tacked over the window to prevent curious eyes from looking inside. The opposition to the lamp was not wholly and entirely, after all, a matter of obstinacy or dislike of change. They had their weight in deciding the question, but there was one drawback, equally recognised by both, but now slowly emerging in the confession of Jamie. He did not use it as an argument—the argumentative stage had been passed. It was an explanation.

My three brothers had gone away, one after another, to push their fortunes in other parts. They seldom wrote. Two had to get others to do it, anyway, and the third had a family and cares enough of his own. One of the gentle delusions of that far-off life in Pogue's Entry was connected with the burning candles that nightly lit up our cottage, and beside which Jamie worked at his trade.

A bright little shining spark about the size of a pin-head would occasionally appear on the burning wick. To us poor folk it was like a little star in a fairy firmament. It was always a harbinger of hope, the forerunner of good news from abroad. It was a sure sign that a letter was on the way. Anna believed it, so did Jamie, so did we all. We would as soon have doubted our very existence. Just as the rainbow was God's sign in the heavens that never again would the world be destroyed by flood, so the bright little spark in the candle was the mystical sign that after all we were not forgotten!

'I was thinkin' of it all the time, myself,' Anna said.

'I hate t' give it up,' said Jamie, 'for it's been a more saucy comfort t' me than I ever let on!'

While it was yet dark I was awakened by the sound of hammering in the bedroom. As I listened the town clock struck three. I dare not move, of course, but next morning the secret came out.

Together they had stayed up all night and mastered with mutual forbearance and with a good deal of childish glee the mysterious mechanism of our first lamp. As soon as it was 'dacently' permissible, the family gathered around and exulted on the accomplished fact. There it hung, suspended on a temporary nail, awaiting full introduction to its permanent abiding place over the worn bench.

Next night we were bathed in glory! The new lamp was a new social status. Never had we so many visitors; they filled the house, they peered in the window, they wondered how we got it and what we would get next! Jamie was content. Anna was triumphant. She took entire charge of it, but many a time for years afterwards she would turn the lamp out after his work was done, and light the candle in her sconce in the corner. Jamie would smile knowingly. It was for his comfort as much as her own.

Chapter 9

QUARE PEOPLE

I

'Oul' Solomon must haave haad a terrible time wi'
three hundhred ov thim, eh, Jamie?' Baxter said one
night, when the discussion turned on the oddities of
'quare people'.

'Ay,' Jamie said. 'An he must haave haad a
cast-iron constitution, but I think it's a feerie story.
It wud be jist as aisy t' believe that Jonah swallowed
the whale as t' believe that aany maan cud answer
th' questions ov sich a crowd—t' say nothin' ov his
other juties t' thim!'

'It's a mortal wondther that God didn't send a
pirta famine or sumthin', t' rejuce thim t' sinsible
numbers—don't ye think so, Anna?'

'I think,' said Anna, 'that it's more ov a wondther
that he wasn't provided wi' a wise oul' bachelor like
you, Ben, t' keep 'im in th' straight an' narrow path!'

Oh, ay,' Baxter replied; 'shure it's aisy t' see that
ye're in fayvor ov laws that wud allow aany oul'
throllop t' haave a harem-scarum ov as maany wives
as he cud thole, ay, deed, that's aisy seen.'

'I'm no more in fayvor ov two wives than I am ov
two husbands, but it's newins t' hear a woman
blamed for laws good or bad; shure all laws are made
t' poor oul' craithurs who're chiefly entitled to make
them, because they're not women.'

124

'Thry th' weather, Ben,' Jamie said. 'Ye'll haave a betther chance to show off yer powers.'

'Och!' sighed Baxter; 'shure it bangs Bannaghter t' see th' conthrariness ov wimin aanyway.'

'Rubbitch,' said Jamie, 'jist rubbitch!'

'Don't be too hard on him, Jamie,' Anna said. 'Shure all oul' bachelors talk like that till they're married, an' thin—'

'Ay, an' thin,' interrupted Baxter, 'they talk th' teeth out ov a saw.'

Baxter was sitting in his socks, while James was cobbling his old boots. Anna was making waxed ends. When Baxter sat in his socks he was distinguished by an atmosphere that was all his own. We had no vocabulary for odours. To us they were either good or bad, but the specific gravity of Baxter's was of such a nature that it not only taxed our limited language, but wore our good manners to the thinness of a wafer.

Of course, in these scientific days we have the pycnometer, hydrometer, and thermometer. By their aid we can estimate the densities, intensities, values, and qualities of such things, but in those far-off days and in that old-fashioned alley, when a thing arrived at a stage when it created nausea, we just described it as 'a whiff of Baxter'!

It was this odoriferousness that catalogued him with the 'quare' people of our town.

In discussion quare people on this particular evening, Baxter did not mean to be rude, but he interrupted Anna several times, and Jamie had an abrupt and somewhat rough method of fighting for fair play.

'I'll tell ye somethin', Ben,' he said, when his opportunity arrived. 'If ye manured yer mind wi' the

125

same care that ye manure yer socks, ye wudn't be half as quare as folks think ye are!'

'Ye were awful hard on poor Ben,' Anna said, when the house was cleared that night.

'Rubbitch!' said Jamie. 'He's got a wooden skull, Anna, an' nothin' short ov a butcher's cleaver wud make an impression on 'im.'

An impression had been made, however, for Baxter became quite loquacious in giving reminiscences of quare people he had known.

'Ov coorse,' he said, 'a maan isn't quare, jist bekase he cyant whustle wi' a hot pirta in his mouth—is he, Anna?'

'Oh, deed no,' Anna said; 'but it's a throughother mind that makes us do throughother things.' The case of Sammy Fisher was cited. Sammy, in the language of our quarter, was described as 'wantin' a square of bein' round'. One day when about three years of age, I was splashing my hands in the old barrel that stood under the spout and caught the rain-water from the roof. I lost my balance and tumbled into the barrel. Sammy happened along at the moment, and seeing my feet sticking out, he calmly walked in and said:

'Ye known yer wee boy, Jamie, don't ye?'

'Ay,' Jamie said, without stopping his work.

'Well,' said Sammy, 'he's bubblin' away in th' wather wi' his heels sticking out.'

When Jamie arrived I had ceased to 'bubble'. He pulled me out and brought me back to consciousness. Then he looked around for Sammy, who was bending over the fire, warming his hands. Using one of his select theological phrases, he gave Sammy a vicious kick—where it didn't hurt much—and informed him that if he ever darkened the door with his shadow again, he would 'bate' him 'till an inch of his death'.

When Baxter mentioned Sammy's name as being one of the quare ones, Jamie retorted:

'Sammy isn't quare—he's an ijot!'

II

At this juncture McGrath, the rag-man, entered with an empty can in his hand.

'God save ye kindly, one an' all,' was his salutation. He had come to 'borrow' a can of 'good clane wather', to save himself the trouble of going to the town well for it.

'Ay, an' welcome, Mr McGrath,' Anna said. Jist dip yer can in th' crock.' He filled his can and stood for a moment as if hesitating between his wife's needs and his curiosity to know what we were talking about. He was invited to sit down a while and share the crack. Down on the floor he flopped beside his can, and fishing a cutty pipe out of his pocket he lit it at a live turf, and proceeded to enjoy a smoke in three keys.

'We're jist haavin' a crack about quare people,' said Baxter. 'Ye must know quite a wheen ov thim aroun' th' town, eh, McGrath?'

'I do that,' said the rag-man, 'an' I'll bate ye half a bap an' threacle to a hard boiled egg, that I can tell ye at laste wan quare thing about any maan, wuman, or chile, that ye can name—barrin' ov coorse, m'self!'

Heavy footsteps were heard coming down the entry: they were familiar to us, and we rejoiced. It was Withero, the stone-breaker, and he was the only man we knew who was a match for McGrath.

'Man alive,' he said to McGrath, as he scanned the faces of those present; 'ye're a sight for sore eyes. I haven't laid an eye on ye fur a month ov Sundays—where're ye been? Over helpin' th' Queen to rule the Scotch?'

'No, ye're bate!' said McGrath. 'I've been sellin' holy wather t' Orange lodges!'

'Is this a can ov it?'

'Ay, this is a special brand I had sent from Rome fur Johnston ov Ballykillbeg.'

'Well, wud His Holiness object if ye jist made Baxter a prisint ov it t' wash his feet—there's a smell aroun' here that ye cud hing yer hat on!'

'At laste, he might spare a few dhrops t' sprinkle on yer tongue, Withero,' said Baxter.

'Sit down, Willie—sit down an' say somethin' nice fur a change,' said Anna, 'an' don't forget to remember that there's more senses than a sense of humour!'

'Ay, there's a sense ov dacency, Anna; but I wuz behind the doore whin th' wor givin' it out—M' mother—God rest 'er sowl—wuz a dacent wuman, but I tuk afther m' father, ay, I did that, heigh-ho, it's a quare oul' world!'

'Ye must come across quite a wheen ov quare people at yer stone pile, Willie,' said Jamie.

'Ye're a good guesser t' know nothin', Jamie. I haave that, an' I'll tell ye somethin', an' ye needn't let on, bekase it's a sacret—I'm the only maan in th' townland that isn't quare!'

'Well, it's no use joinin' a brass band unless ye can toot yer own horn!' said Baxter.

'Th' do say that ye talk a lot t' yerself, Withero: is that thrue?' asked McGrath.

'It is that,' said Withero, 'but only whin I want a

sinsible audience. Whin I'm not particular aany oul'
fool that comes along is good enough, an' savin' yer
prisince, an' manein' no offince, that's the rayson
I'm always so dacent t' yerself!'

'I say, Anna,' said Jamie, 'these Solomons haave
been aitin' razors fur supper, don't ye think a nice
cup o' tay wud safen th' sharp edges a bit, eh?'

While Anna prepared the tea, Jamie put the
finishing touches to the repairs of Baxter's boots,
and the 'Solomons' continued the flow of compliments.

'Seen oul' Dougall lately?' asked the stone-
breaker.

'Now *there's* a quare maan, if there iver was wan
in th' wurrld,' said Baxter.

'What's quare about Dougall?' asked Jamie.

'Why, man alive,' said Withero, 'he'd blaze like a
tar barrel if ye put a match to his breath.'

'That wudn't make 'im quare,' said Jamie. 'Ye cud
light a baker's dozen ov thim aany day in Darragh's
pub.'

'Isn't a maan quare that swallows a house an' lot
an' th' happiness of his wife an' wains forby.'

'Maybe.'

'Maan, Jamie, ye don't need t' be stark starin'
mad t' be quare!'

'Ach, stop yer blitherin', Willie, who's th' judge
ov who's quare an' who isn't? You're quare bekase
ye've nayther chick nor chile, I'm quare bekase I've
got sich a terrible lot ov childther. Th' vicar's quare
bekase he won't let Orange flags on th' church
steeple, oul' John Kirk's quare bekase he's a
Presbyterian, an' a Home Ruler, wee Misther
McTammany goes along th' streets jinglin' his kays
an' tossin' thim in th' air, and Lord Massereene'd

rether haave a ride wi' wan ov th' Drummonds on a side cyar than ride behind a coachman in a tall hat an' buff breeches. Shure th' whole thing's so throughother that nobody knows who's quare an' who's an ijot! It's jist balderdash—let's talk about somethin' we can ait!'

'Oh, ay; but ye didn't mention oul' Docther Taggart, Jamie,' said Baxter. 'Th' whole town thinks he's quare bekase whether ye've got a sore head, a broken ankle, a jumpin' toothache, or the yellow jaundice, he gives ye a double dose ov salts an' seeney! Now can ye bate that fur quareness, eh, Jamie?'

'No,' Jamie replied, 'I can't bate it, but I'm jist a shure as gun's iron that I'm the only maan in th' town that isn't quare. Now put that in yer pipes an' smoke it—how's that tay gettin' on, Anna?'

'Ye wudn't like t' settle th' question first—wud ye, dear?'

'Not by a jugful! That will take jist about a million years, an' ye can't steep tay that long an' enjoy it!'

By the time the tea was handed around, Baxter's boots were finished, and on his feet. The thermometer would have recorded the fact if we had had one, but we hadn't. We were nevertheless appreciative of the change. We youngsters did not relish all this palaver about the quareness of mere humans. The quare antics of fairies, gnomes, fiends, and angels were more to our liking, and we hoped that Anna or the rag-man would give us a fairy or a ghost story before Jamie gave the neighbours the pointed hint that we needed what remained of the candle to light us to bed.

We were not fond of Baxter. He was too matter-of-fact—always provoking discussion over things that didn't matter. We hoped the tea would change the programme, but it didn't. We watched Withero drain his cup to the very dregs. We hoped he would read our fortunes in the straggling tea-leaves at the bottom, but he didn't. Instead, he rolled off another list of quare people, and told us of their failings and foibles.

'Ye wor spakin' ov Dougall,' he said. 'Well, now, it's thrue he dhrunk himself out ov house an' home, wife an' wains, until he had nayther mate, money, nor marbles, nor chalk t' make th' ring. Whin he got t' th' bottom, he did more quare things, but a laste wan o' these quare antics had a sauncy result.'

'Oh, th' quare men wor not all behind th' doore whin th' wit wuz bein' handed out,' said Baxter.

'As I wuz sayin',' the stone-breaker continued, 'wan night Dougall didn't know where ur how t' raise th' wind—he'd got t' the wall at th' world's end, an' he'd his back up agin it. He wuz so thirsty that he disremembered his name. He wuz sittin' on th' wall ov Misthress Mulholland's pig-sty, scratchin' his head an' switherin' t' bate th' divil, when an idea got intil 'im.

'Th' ceilin' ov Tomson's tap-room wuz crack't an' baggy in th' middle, Dougall wuz a good plastherer, ye mind, so down he goes. A wheen ov oul' throllops wor settlin' the affairs ov th' universe in high dudgeon.

' "What d'ye want?" says oul' Tomson, wi' a knowin' luk at Dougall.

' "I'm lukin fur McConkey," says he, "an' I know he isn't here, but he's comin'." Up gits an oul' *caillach* frum Muckamore, an' starts t' sing "Croppies lie down". Dougall kep' his eye on th' ceilin'. The singin' wuz so bad that oul' Tomson wuz

131

furyus. He winked Dougall out t' th' back doore, an', says he, "If ye'll stuff a hot pirta in that ass's mouth," sez he, "ye'll haave a glass ov th' best on th' shelf."

' "Haave ye a hot pirta?" sez Dougall.

' "I haave."

' "I'm yer maan," sez Dougall. Jist then there wuz a divil ov a rumpus inside. A couple of papists in Bow Lane had changed th' musical programme. Dougall's throat remained as dry as a whistle, but he kep' his eye on th' ceilin'.

'Afther a while, whin all their tongues wor waggin', widout rhyme ur rayson—an' Tomson's whiskey had melted th' wits out o' their skulls, oul' McIntosh, ov Patey's Lane, wuz lifted ontil th' long bench an' nothin' wud do but he'd hev t' recite th' Battle ov Scyarva! Dougall stud be th' doore wid his eye glued t' th' ceilin'. McIntosh wuz dhrunk in th' legs, frum th' knees down, an' jist cudn't balance himself on sich threacherous undtherpinnin'. Whin th' oul' fella dhropped in a heap, up steps me bould Dougall. "Chaps," sez he, "I haaven't recited since I wuz th' size of a ragweed, but if ye can procure me an Admiral's three-cornered hat an' a good cavalry sword, I'll fayvor ye wid Shakespeare's famous pom, Balaclava."

' "We're short on naval outfits," sez Misther Tomson, "but ye can haave an oul' cavalry sword," sez he, "that cut th' liver an' lights out ov a rebel in '98."

'While oul' Tomson wint fur th' sword Dougall fixed a chair undther the place where th' ceilin' bagged most. Sword in han' he gowled thru th' pom till he aruv at th' excited part. Thin he bellow'd like a Moylena bull:

' ' Into th' valley ov death—into th' mouth ov hell—
Galloped th' six hundthred!''

an' wid that he hit th' ceilin' a skite wid th' sword,
an' down it came wid a crash!'

'Egad, I'll bate th' oul' spulpan got th' job ov
plastherin' it up!' said Baxter.

'He did that,' replied Withero. 'But isn't th'
quareness ov a quare maan th' quarest conundrum in
a quare wurrld!'

III

A door closed with a bang. We knew it was
McGrath's door just opposite ours.

'I'll be hung, dhrawn, an' quarthered,' said
McGrath, 'if that isn't oul' Jane comin' afther her
wather.'

A moment later the rag-man's wife opened the
door and entered.

She looked like a wet hen. Her hair was
disordered, and she had forgotten to put all her
clothes on. Jamie said afterwards that she looked as
if she had been dragged both ways through a hedge.

The teacups attracted her attention.

'Much good may it do ye,' she said, looking at
Anna. Then she turned on her husband with an
expression of contempt and said:

'When ye want t' sit like a clockin' hen an' cackle
yer head off—why don't ye be civil enough t' let on?'

'Here's th' wather, Jane,' said her husband. 'Take
it an' give yer bitther tongue a holiday!'

'I'm sorry, Mrs McGrath,' said Anna, 'but ye see
these wise men do be thinkin' long t' show off their
wits before wan another.'

'Ay, dear, yer sorely thried yerself, I don't misdoubt, but ye see I've been sittin' in m' shift fur hours waitin' fur th' oul' baste, an' while I wuz sittin' shiverin' like a lafe on a three, there wuz a rappin' at th' back windy—an' I do believe it wuz th' ghost of Liza Wallace, fur afther th' rappin' there wuz a strong smell ov bad fish—jist like oul' Liza, God rest her soul.'

'Come over here into th' corner, dear,' said Anna, 'an' haave a good strong cup o' hot tay—it'll warm ye up.'

'God-love-ye-Anna,' said Mrs McGrath, between her loud sups, 'how d'ye stand so maany men comin' an' goin' all th' time?'

'Well, dear, ye know it wudn't be all curds an' whey if it wuzn't fur th' fact that Jamie and me earn our livin' by improvin' their undtherstandin'.'

Mrs McGrath didn't see the point, but ventured the suggestion that 'there wasn't nothin' they needed so much'.

'They've been palaverin' about quare people,' Anna said, 'but I noticed that all th' quare people they talked about were men.'

'Throth, I hear they're doublin' th' men's ward in th' asylum,' said Mrs McGrath—'a wink like that shud be as good as a nod to a blind horse, eh, Anna?'

'Ay, but th' throuble is, dear, ye can only wink at some men wi' an axe.'

'Rubbich!' said Jamie.

'Worse nor rubbich!' said Baxter.

Anna laughed, and Mrs McGrath increased the noise of her supping.

'It's only among ijots that men are two t' wan,' said McGrath. 'Among quare people th' wimin are four t' wan, ay, th' are that, jist as shure as wather runs an' grass grows!'

'Livin' wi' quare men, how cud th' privint it, Tam?' said his wife.

'Jane,' said Tam, 'ye haave a fine tongue for clippin' hedges—'

The light went out. Jamie was snuffing the candle with his thumb and forefinger, but had gripped it too low and extinguished it.

'Where wuz Mozes whin th' light went out?' said Baxter. A piece of paper was folded and lit at the burning turf. Anna handed it to McGrath, and he passed it on to Jamie. As the big tallow candle blazed up, Anna said so softly:

'Now God be thanked fur light.'

On that there was no comment. It was one of those touches of tender mysticism that always smoothed out for the moment our roughness. How strangely thin that veil that divided the seen from the unseen! How near laughter to tears, and the uncouthness of untrained tongues to the most refined things of the spirit.

The work of the day over, Jamie set the big candlestick in the midst, and turned his face towards the glow of the burning peat. That was the signal to us that the gentle hint to the neighbours to take their leave would soon be forthcoming, and when they were gone Anna would draw up the table, and we would have the last 'bite' of the day together.

Tam McGrath, feeling that the man had been rather worsted in the endless theme, spread his legs out on the floor and wound up the night's discussion with a story of a quare woman.

IV

'D'ye mind Johnny Gerner, ov Killead?' he asked.

'Oh, I mind him rightly,' Jamie said.

135

'He was a quare maan, if iver there wuz wan,' said McGrath, 'an' so wuz his wife, but she was the quarest ov th' two. We lived forninst thim years agone. Johnny wuz a great maan fur the fife and dhrum, an, a terrible hater ov the papishes. He jist lived fur the glory ov wearin' a sash on th' twelfth an' bein' a chaplain; he carried th' Bible of his lodge in all their doin's. In money matthers he wuz close-fisted, an' in matthers ov religion as narrow as a hen's face—ay, 'deed there wuzn't a closer-fisted maan between Anthrim an' Donaghadee.'

'An' I'm th' boy that knows it,' said Withero. 'Johnny had a big body, but his wee sowl wud haave had as much room in a thimble as a bumbee wud in Lough Neagh. Ay, that's Johnny Gerner, of Killead.'

'His wife's father wuz a papish an' her mother wuz a Protestant,' continued McGrath, but Maggie wuz nayther nor didn't want to be. She'd jist as soon wear a sprig ov shamrock on the seventeenth as an orange bow on the 12th, but Johnny smiled at th' bow and girned at th' shamrock. She never had a ha'penny she cud call her own. Wan day she thought she'd thry t' bamboozle him out ov a shillin' ur two. She up and towld Johnny she wanted t' buy a shift. He said he'd buy it. She said no man that iver stepped in black leather boots wud buy a shift fur her. "Thin," sez he, "Ye'll go without."

'Wan night whin Johnny came home he found a shillin' lyin' on th' table in th' front room.

' "Where did that come frum?" sez he.

' "Th' man above only knows," sez she, "but I shudn't wondther if Bob Coyle didn't lave it. He wuz here this afthernoon."

' "What wuz he here fur?"

' "Well now, dear knows, except jist t' see how all th' worrld an' his wife was thratin' Maggie Gerner?"

' "What fur shud he lave a shillin'?"

' "I dunno, but bein' an oul' friend o' mine I did up an' tell him th' God Almighty thruth that frum wan year's end t' th' other I hadn't a shillin' t' call m' own—ay, 'deed I did that!'

' "What did ye give 'im fur th' shillin'?"

Th' brute baste!' said Mrs McGrath.

'Whisht yer noise! said McGrath, as he looked disapprovingly at his wife, and proceeded.

'Maggie gowl'd as if her heart wud split in two, but Johnny was as could as a stepmother's breath. Nixt mornin' he wuz still in th' tanthrum. Whilst aitin' his breakfast he tuk th' shillin', toss't it in th' air, catch't it, an' slapp'd it on th' table. Not a wurrd did he spake. Ivery two ur three sups ov tay he tuk he'd toss up an' slap down th' shillin'. First th' noise wuz like hittin' a barn doore wi' yer fist. Thin he larned how t' make a sharp cuttin' noise b' clickin' it. He click't at breakfast, he click't at supper. First th' clickin' hurt her ears, thin it hurt her brains, thin it hurt her heart. Ivery click seemed louder nor th' last wan. Sometimes th' craither heard th' clickin' all day long. Sometimes she'd hear it in a nightmare, an' wake up wid a cream.

'Fur two whole calendther years he didn't spake a wurrd till her. Whin he'd be forced t' spake, he'd write it on a slip ov paper. He kept th' bed. She lay on a shakedown be the fire. Ivery day wuz like ivery other—jist the raspin', gratin' sound of click, click, click.

'She thried t' make him spake, but she might as well haave thried t' stick a plasther on a hedgehog. Wan day she tuk a hatchet an' chop't up the table.

137

He didn't bate her, he jist kept on clickin' on th' dhresser. She made kindlin' ov th' dhresser, an' he click't it on a stool. She stapp't goin' out. She wudn't comb her hair, she wudn't cook his males nor wash his shirt, nor nothin'. He niver laid a han' on her. He jist kept on clickin', clickin', clickin'.

'Wan day she dhres't up an' wint till th' poorhouse, an ax'd to be taken intil the asylum fur th' mad.

' "But yer not mad," sez Misther Garder.

' "But I'm goin'," sez she.

' "We cyant take ye till ye're gone," sez he.

'Well, it's a long lane that hes no turnin'. Wan day Johnny wuz puttin' a coat ov thatch on Misthress Curtin's cottage, an' he fell off th' roof an' broke his neck.'

'God he thank't fur that,' said Mrs McGrath.

'It's betther nor bein' hung,' said Baxter.

Turning to Anna, McGrath said:

'Now what wud ye think Maggie Gerner did, eh' Anna?'

'Dear knows,' Anna said. 'Maybe she jist washed up an' begun life all over again.'

'I'll bate a ha'penny she said, "Good riddance t' bad rubbich," ' said Baxter.

'What wud ye say, Jamie?'

'Ax me somethin' aisy,' said Jamie. 'Shure only God cud tell what a wuman wud do, an' He isn't always shure.'

'Well,' said McGrath, as he knocked the ashes out of his pipe, 'ov all th' animals that wint into th' ark, wuman wuz th' quarest, ay, as shure as rent day she wuz. She sowld th' house an' garden, and wi' th' money bought a fine headstone ov the kind that quality puts up. She hed big goold letthers on it: "In

138

lovin' mimory ov John Gerner, erected by his devoted an' sorrowin' wife." An' down at th' bottom she hed: *Not lost, but gone before.*'

Late that night, when the neighbours had all gone, Jamie and Anna sat by the fire talking over the strange case of the Gerners. Opinions were divided as to which of them was the quarest. To the mind of Jamie, Mrs Gerner was by long odds the quarest of the two. When rather worsted in the argument he just ended the quiet colloquy by saying:

'Well, she bate the divil.'

'Ay, dear,' said Anna, 'an' that wuz her intintion!'

Chapter 10

HIMSELF

I think I see Anna in the fair fields of
heaven, and Jamie—*safely arrived*
                                        Jane Barlow

I

Jane seems to have had an idea that Jamie had a
hard time in getting there—and he had. Any one
who held that opinion, received it from Jamie
himself.

There is no hard and fixed line of demarcation
between the dialect of the north and that of the
south. Expressive words and phrases have a way of
travelling beyond the domain of their origin. Very
often when referring to Jamie, Anna would simply
say, 'Himself'. When met on the street and asked
how *everything* was at home, Jamie would reply,
'She's all right!' These words and phrases were more
common in the south, but they were familiar too in
the north.

When Nature was fashioning Jamie, she intended
to give him the appearance of an oak, but she
dropped into a reverie and while swithering over it
changed her mind, and gave him the appearance of a
cedar instead. He always looked to me like a cedar
whose branches had an arrested development—
cropped rather close to the trunk, and scantily
clothed with foliage.

A cedar exposed to wintry blasts, wraps its roots the more tightly around the rocks and battles for standing room, and the fiercer the struggle the more rugged the appearance. He was of medium physical proportions. He had a rugged face, seamed and scarred by time and care. He had a pyramidal nose and a strong, firm mouth.

The special feature of the homely, kind face was the eyes. They were of a grayish blue. They were windows through which we could all look into his mind and tell with certainty it varying moods. There were times when they looked like live coals and at other times they were full of an ineffable tenderness.

He had a voice that could be full of thunder. It was rarely that. Mostly it had a soft, purring sound, and irresistible in its appeal. In laughter he couldn't shake the floor for it was made of mud, but he shook the bench and shook himself in every fibre of his being. He had a limited vocabulary, and was usually unfortunate in his selection of phrases, but to accuse him of profanity would have been an insult. He could punctuate his conversation with expletives which exploded, in what, to him, was mere emphasis, but which to others of a wider range of words would appear profane.

He had no theological views, but some very definite ideas about religion. To keep the Sabbath as rigorously as the Pharisees, to do good work, make reasonable charges, and keep out of debt were cardinal things to him. All questions of a theological nature he referred to Anna. He did this at first as a means of escape, but later because he enjoyed the ease with which she confounded the sermon tasters and theological experts.

He established a standing threat to 'whale hell'

out of any of us who whistled or played shinny on Sunday. We never feared him—not even when he added a little lightning to this thunder.

The Queen was, to him, the acme of human perfection, but he vowed that he would refuse to mend even her boots after twelve o'clock on Saturday night. This dogmatism on the Sabbath did not appeal to Anna, and occasionally she would suggest that 'the Sabbath was made for man and not man for the Sabbath'.

'I don't care a damn what it was made for, Anna,' he would reply, 'the Sabbath's the Sabbath, an' forby, how am I t' know what the thing was made for?' He went to church a dozen times, but each time he had a good excuse. On these occasions he attended the baptisms of one of his own children. He 'glunched' (complained) a good deal about these functions, because he had to bow to the superior knowledge of Anna, and put on a dickey.

'Botheration,' he would say, 'I hate the —— things, it's like rehearsin' for th' gallows!' In such extreme agony Anna would remind him of his own pet phrase—one he wore threadbare to folks in trouble. 'Thole it an' bate it!'

II

He donned a dickey once to attend the funeral of a Catholic neighbour. It so annoyed him that he brought it home in his pocket.

'It's a scandal, dear,' Anna said.

'Ay, of course it is,' he sneered, 'but there was one man who agreed with me!'

'Who, in pity's name?'

'Th' corpse!'

143

'How do ye know?'

His wife tould me that his last words were: 'Don't bury me with a dickey on—if ye do I'll come back from purgatory and frighten the soul out o' ye!'

On one occasion, when discussing the question of an after-life, Jamie said:

'If I iver get there, it'll be just because I'm her husband.' As he spoke, he jerked his thumb in the direction of the chimney corner.

'An' supposin',' said Anna, 'th' send me to the other place, Jamie?'

'Well, in that case,' he said, 'it wouldn't be hell at all, at all!'

At his work on the bench he sang a good deal. He sang when he was merry and he sang when he was sad. 'Black-eyed Susan' was one of his favourite ballads. When I took a pair of boots to a customer and returned without the price, he would express himself in song:

Och, it's a wondtherful world t' live in,
T' lend or spend or give in,
But t' beg or borrow or git wan's own,
Shure it's th' worst ould world that iver was known!'

The religious feuds of Ireland were of less interest to Jamie than to any Irishman I ever knew. All sorts of men and women aired their views on current topics to him. He heard all, and argued with very few. Those who have to sit barefooted in a cobbler's shop until their boots are mended are not usually the best informed in the community, and Jamie knew that. With wild vagaries he was tolerant—not that his business interests demanded diplomacy. He knew his customers were 'jist bletherin' ' to pass away the time.

Sometimes he would strike a postive note.

'When ye show me a man who is happier because he hings his hat up in a particular place o' Sundays, or because o' th' colour ov the cockade he wears, it'll be time enough fur me t' take a han'.'

'Ay, oh ay,' Ben Baxter said in answer to that, one day, 'but how'd ye like t' live undther th' rule ov a Pope, Jamie?'

'That's blether, Ben; it's worse nor blether, it's a ha'penny pistol cocked in people's faces, until they come t' believe it's a loaded revolver. It's the blether ov a parrot or a magpie whose tongue has bin split wi' a sixpence. If th' Queen lived at wan end ov th' street, an' the Pope at th' other, it wouldn't make onny difference t' me. Their oul' boots wud niver come down our entry t' git mended. No, 'deed they wudn't!'

Anna confessed that she missed most what she had never possessed. With Jamie it was different. The ordinary pleasures of civilised man he never knew and never craved. He never saw a play, never attended a concert. There were occasional summer excursions, he never took such an outing. He could neither read nor write. Art, literature, drama, music, and their uplifting influence, were things he scarcely ever heard of, much less enjoyed. Of course, there were others, many of them, nearly a townful of them.

His workshop was also our dining and living room. It measured about twelve by fourteen feet.

There was no room for furniture, even if there had been money to buy it. The old shelf had more broken crockery on it than it had of whole. The walls were white-washed, and a few ornaments sat on the old yellow mantelshelf over the fireplace.

145

His life was one of unrelieved toil—toil for less, much less, than what other poor folks called 'the bare necessities'.

If we had been asked why he continued to carry on, day after day, year in year out, I think he would have looked toward Anna, as he always did when he was puzzled, and would have expected her to answer the question. If forced to answer it himself, he would have enumerated the pleasures of life. They were very real to him. Sorrow was an intruder—a temporary visitor at most. His will to live was based on love. The out-working of that love was a perfect understanding between them. The coming of the children, so many of them, one after another, added to his interest in life. Each of them brought a hope. Often these hopes were at low ebb, but there were always enough live ones to give new interests.

I am sure that in making up a debit and credit account he would have omitted many things of importance. When reminding Anna, as he did often, of the early years of married life, a strangely beautiful light was in his eyes. Memory, therefore, consciously or unconsciously, was a strong factor, and bound him more closely to the supreme object of his tenderest solicitude. He had a few friends. They came on Sundays and occasionally at other times, and brought the news of their own particular little worlds.

III

Sunday was not only visiting day, it was shaving day too, and for that Jamie needed half the whole house. One of my brothers brought home a sporting paper once, and in it was a full-paged picture of a roped enclosure with two prize-fighters in the centre.

146

'Now that's the kind o' thing ye need, Jamie,' Anna said, showing it to him.

'What fur?'

'T' shave in!'

'Oh, no,' he said, with a thin smile, 'I don't need the space, but I'd like to hire them two husky fellahs t' keep m' family in ordther while I'm shavin'!'

He had a shaving temperament. It was the occasion when all the acerbities in his nature came to the surface. His paraphernalia was like a midshipman's chest—everything on top and nothing handy.

Within a space of about seven by nine feet he must have walked miles during each shave—from the kettle hanging on the chain to the bit of broken mirror in the front window—to the strap on the south wall—to the tub in which he steeped his leather—to and fro, back and forth, sputtering, puffing, stropping, and lathering over and over again. If he cut himself, he would blame it on us, or on the razor, and talk as if he were bleeding to death! If we giggled, we took good care to do it outside.

'I don't think the Almighty can be plazed with yer galavantin' aroun' th' house on Sunday mornin' with a bad temper in yer heart an' a razor in yer hand, Jamie!' Anna once said.

'Oh, yer quite mistook!' Jamie said. 'He's highly plazed!'

'Why?'

'Because it says in the Bible that cleanliness is next t' godliness!'

'Oh, no, it doesn't!'

'Well, since ye know sich an awful heap, what diz it say?'

'What about?'

'Shavin'!'

147

'Nothin'! Except that wimin mustn't!'

'Yer jist foolin'.'

'Dear knows I'm not.'

'Ha! ha!' Jamie laughed; 'that's a good joke on God!'

'What us?'

'Tellin' a woman not to shave. Bad scran to it all. I'll bate He did that jist because he know'd rightly it wuz th' only Commandment that a woman wud iver willingly obey!'

Anna was an adept in smoothing over difficulties, either our own or those of our neighbours. There were some that baffled her. Jamie had little tact. He was very blunt. One night I fell asleep in front of the fire. When I awoke I knew it was long past my time. Dreading to be sent aloft to my attic, I feigned sleep and kept still. They were discussing a problem, the solution of which was handed over to Jamie.

In the next entry there lived a young unmarried woman who had two children. Failing in health, she could no longer work for them. The father of one of the children was quite able to help her, but she was too proud to ask aid from one who had thrown her aside.

Anna told Jamie the whole story, and he was so wroth that he determined to act.

'Yer words are too saft, Anna,' he said, 'th' spulpan needs a man t' read th' riot act. Th' baste has no conscience at all, that ye cud appeal to. Let me handle him!'

So between them they staged a one-act play. On a Sunday afternoon the house was cleared. We were all sent off. The old folks only remained. In the space usually occupied by the work-bench, a basket of turf dust or coom was scattered over the mud floor.

In the coom had been scattered a handful of peas. For a hungry child this was a device for what was called 'divartin' th' hunger'. When there were several children the scramble to find the peas was diversion while there was a pea to be found, but in the staged play one little fellow had a monopoly. He was just about three, and when shown how to find the peas he was taken over into the corner.

As Peter McGonigal's steps were heard at the door, the boy was given the freedom of the coom pile again. Peter was given a seat where he could see every movement of the child. When the weather and the crops had been discussed, the child became the centre of interest.

'Th' wee fella acts as if he cud ate a man off his horse!' said Peter.

'Ay, he diz that,' Jamie said, 'an' shure there isn't a thrush's ankle o' nourishment in th' heap. What's a gopen (handful) of pays?'

'It's like a daisy in a bull's mouth!' Peter replied, with evident sympathy.

'An' t' think that th' poor chile should starve jist because he came into th' world without proper credentials,' Anna added.

'Whose chile is he?' asked Peter.

'A neighbour's—a poor craither who hasn't a leg t' stand on fur wakeness.'

'Man alive, it's the throughother world we live in!' said the unsuspecting villain of the piece.

It was Anna's part to tell the story. She spoke quietly and told of a girl's brave fight against great odds. She told of the unmarried mother's struggle to support the unnamed child, and she told it in such a way that it turned into whatever conscience there was to work on.

'The curse of Cromwell on such a brute of a Turk!' hissed Peter, between his clenched teeth.

'An' if she wuz your sister, Pether, what would ye do to him?' Jamie asked.

'Me, Jamie. Me? I'd hammer th' baste t' death be inches! I wud that, even if I had to hing fer it!'

Anna took the baby boy from the floor and placed it on Peter's knee.

'Cheer up, wee maan,' Peter said; 'there's a good time comin'.'

'Ay,' Anna said, with a touch of irony, 'an' when the sky falls we'll all catch larks!' There was a harshness in his voice and fire in his eyes when Jamie said:

'Pether McGonigal, *you* are the father ov the chile on yer lap!'

'Holy Mother ov God!' he gasped. There was deathly silence. No one spoke. Peter hung his head. Jamie and Anna went out and left him there. Five minutes later he came out with the boy in his arms and carried him to his mother.

That night, just as the curfew ceased tolling, Molly Conner noiselessly entered, and sitting down on the floor beside Anna, laid her head on her lap and wept—wept in joy and gratitude.

IV

The time came when they were left almost alone. Most of us were scattered over the world. One married daughter only remained, living at times in the old home, and at other times in a home of her own. During the last years of Anna's life, Jamie softened and mellowed. His hair, though still shocky, was as white as snow. For nearly sixty years he had worked in a sitting posture, and the bent body seemed to refuse to straighten up. The stone-breaker left a gap when he went. The sweep went later, so did John Conlon and Sam Johnson, and a lot of others. Old and dear familiar faces no longer smiled in the glow of our peat fire. Nights became lonely—lonely and almost silent now.

One final sensation came at this period. Jamie scraped together for weeks and months enough money to furnish the one surprise of their later life. His power to work diminished, but their needs were few. Every market day he was seen around the second-hand furniture stall in the market-place. He asked the price of various things. The stall-keeper was very kind. He imagined the old man was becoming 'quare in his mind'.

One day he disgorged a few shillings he had hoarded, and made his purchase—carrying it as tenderly home as if it had been the ark of the covenant. It was a chair for Anna!

'Whose is it, dear?' she asked, as he fixed it in her corner.

'Ah, wuman, whose d'ye think, now?'

'Ye haavn't borrowed it, Jamie?'

'Divil a borrow—I've bought it, an' paid fur it, an' it's yours, an', d'ye know, I'd swither a good deal before I'd let the Queen sit in it! Ay, I wud that!'

It was cosy, comfortable, and not out of keeping with its surroundings. A chippendale in rough ash. It was the one luxury of her life.

She laughed with joy over it until she wept. Nothing that Jamie had ever done gave him greater pleasure. He was proud of it. Sometimes, as they had their cup of tea together, she would make him sit in it. He would refuse and hold out. Then she wouldn't

touch her tea until he complied. That would always get him.

'Jamie, dear,' she said one night, 'I feel an awful regret runnin' through m' mind sometimes.'

'You'll be thinkin' long fur the childther, eh?'

'No, not that.'

'Fur th' ould times?'

'No.'

'I'm bate!'

'I do be thinkin' long fur th' ould friends who are gone just t' haave a look at m' new chair!'

Jamie laughed and said:

'Well, now, that reminds me. While I wus waitin' fur the last shillin' fur th' chair—ye see I had an eye on it long before—I had a quare drame wan night. I thought I saw Withero sitting in your chair in th' corner, an', ov coorse, he wuz reg'latin' th' affairs ov th' universe as usual, but he says to me in a cross-grained sort ov way, "So ye waited till I wuz gone before ye got a chair, did ye, an' cock up th' like o' ye to be apin' th' quality just as soon as yer friends is laid undther th' sod. Ay, but I'm here, ye see, an' I'll be here iv'ry night now—jist put that in yer pipe an' smoke it!" I forget th' rest ov his capers, but it wuz quare, wuzn't it?'

'Ay, dear knows, dreams are quare, Jamie, but a great man once said that we're jist th' kind o' stuff that they're made of, an' if Willie can come back, you an' me can, can't we?'

'The Man above only knows, Anna.'

'I will go first, Jamie, but I will return, maybe in a dream, maybe in th' spirit, but—'

'Don't talk about it, Anna, I can't thole it, plaze don't.'

'Oh, don't glunch, dear,' she said, as she took his

153

rough hand in hers. 'We've got to talk about these things, forby, I'll tell ye somethin' nice. Listen now. When we're both beyond the mists, an' there's no more cookin' or mendin' ould boots, I'll tell ye what we'll do! We'll come back in th' summer evenings and go all through the castle gardens!'

'Ha, ha!' he laughed, 'shure ye're jist dotin'!'

'When they're all gone t' bed in th' castle,' she continued, 'we'll invite our friends, Withero, O'Hare, Mary McDonagh, John Conlon, an' our own childther who are over there an' here too, an' we'll haave a fine party in th' big parlour.'

'Not Withero,' Jamie said, 'he'd spit on the carpets!'

'Spirits don't spit, Jamie!'

'Oh, well, ax him!'

'Then we'll slide over th' nice grass lawns and play with the flowers. On Sundays we'll go to church and sit in his lordship's pew.'

'Ay,' Jamie interrupted, 'he'll be out shooting!'

'Is everybody quality over there?' he asked in a half serious tone.

'Oh, bless yer heart, ye needn't swither aany over that. Beyond the clouds th' bigger th' love th' bigger th' quality. There'll be no puttin' on airs, or lettin' on yer somebody when ye're nobody. We'll all wear th' same kind o' clothes, an' eat th' same food.'

'What'll we ate?' Jamie asked. She laughed, and said:

'I dunno, but whatever we ate it'll be nice. Maybe we'll haave friend sunshine and fur tay we'll haave rose-leaves stewed in dew that the angels gather off the violets.'

An' sup mist porridge with forks made ov lightning, eh, Anna?'

'And they laughed together like children.

Then came a period of darkness for Jamie, which was followed by an almost total eclipse. In his own words, 'she faded away like the laves on th' trees'. Her days were few, and she spent them in pain, and in preparing Jamie for the inevitable. He attended her himself. He was full of hope, and refused to believe that she was going. He had grown somewhat deaf, and when he couldn't hear and wouldn't ask her to repeat what he missed, it was torture beyond words. At last he could only hold her hand and read her thoughts. Her feeblest whisper could have been heard and repeated by others, but that was not the same, and when her hand had pressed his for the last time, and the lovelight had gone out of her eyes for ever, he was stupefied.

They took him away from the bedside. The firstborn son returned. There was no light in the window now, nor light in the house. The neighbours came, the carpenter came, the minister came, and Jamie watched them all in silence—with a dazed look in his pain-stricken face.

A turf fire was built that night and the watchers gathered around it. About midnight tea was made. He was urged to have a cup. He refused. Suddenly he arose, asked for a cup of tea, and entering the room of death, closed the door behind him. Silence reigned amongst the watchers. Jamie's voice broke the stillness in broken, husky accents: he was heard to plead:

'Anna, dear, ye'll share a cup fur the last time—jist a cup—God love ye—spake t' me, Anna—spake jist wan last wurd before—ax God t' let ye luk at me an' share this last—'

The firstborn entered to take him away.

'Go away,' Jamie thundered. 'T'morra ye'll take her away an' put her under th' sod, but t'night she's mine—jist mine—go away!'

And awe-stricken, they left him there with his dead.

A month after the burial of Anna the sexton of the parish church saw Jamie rolling a big boulder along a pathway of the graveyard. The perspiration was pouring down his face, his hair was dishevelled by the effort. No one ever knew where he got it. When at the head of the new-made grave he mopped his brow with his sleeve and rested.

Somebody painted two letters on the stone, and he went to wait. He waited longer than he expected, and much longer than he wanted.

'How are you, Jamie?' a neighbour asked one day.

'I'm jist futtherin' aroun' till th' lay me beside 'er in the churchyard,' he answered.

The old chimney corner was now all his own. He sat on her chair, and used her cup and saucer. His dreams sleeping and waking were of her. He could talk of little else. He was like a man whose 'flittin' ' (furniture) had gone on ahead to the new home, while he remained in the empty house. He slept much, and his ability to work had vanished with his desire to live.

One night before the end came he seemed to be on the border, and in his sleep muttered:

'Ye seem to be purty nice quality over there! Ay, ay, well, nobody's got a dickey on—I couldn't thole it, Anna—a dickey's no shirt for an honest maan, aither dead ur alive.'

When he awoke he was told what he had said.

'Well,' he said, smiling, 'yer mother said that all our good dhrams come thrue. Maybe mine will, ay, maybe it will, maybe it'll come thrue in a day ur two.'

In a few hours after that he had solved the great mystery, and God, whom he had described as 'a rale Gintleman', treated him kindly, I am sure.